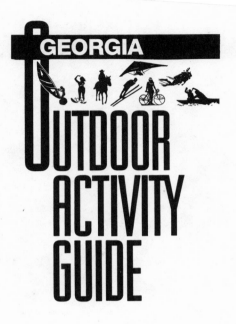

GEORGIA

OUTDOOR ACTIVITY GUIDE

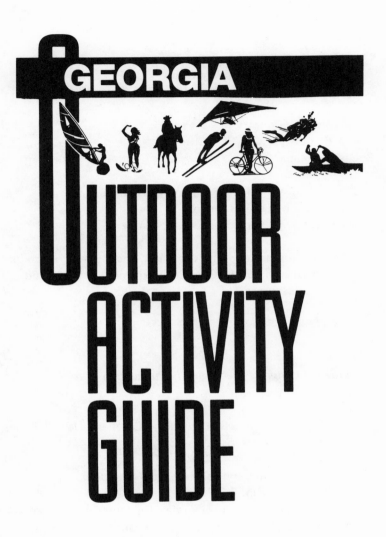

GEORGIA

OUTDOOR ACTIVITY GUIDE

Carol Thalimer and Dan Thalimer

Illustrated by Dale Swensson

Country Roads Press
CASTINE • MAINE

Georgia Outdoor Activity Guide

Published by Country Roads Press
P.O. Box 286, Lower Main Street
Castine, Maine 04421

Text and cover design by Studio 3, Ellsworth, Maine.
Illustrations by Dale Swensson.
Typesetting by Typeworks, Belfast, Maine.

Accommodations and Activities Chart, pages 22–23, reproduced
with permission of the Georgia Department of Parks and
Natural Resources.

ISBN 1-56626-051-5

Library of Congress Cataloging-in-Publication Data

Thalimer, Carol.
    Georgia outdoor activity guide / Carol and Dan Thalimer :
illustrator, Dale Swensson.
        p.   cm.
    Includes bibliographical references and index.
    ISBN 1-56626-051-5 : $9.95
    1. Outdoor recreation—Georgia—Guidebooks. 2. Sports—
Georgia—Guidebooks. 3. Georgia—Guidebooks.   I. Thalimer,
Dan. II. Title.
    GV191.42.G4T43   1994
    796.5′09758—dc20
                                                                93-50901
                                                                    CIP

Printed in the United States of America.
10 9 8 7 6 5 4 3 2 1

*To Bill Schemmel,
Southern gentleman*

CONTENTS

ACKNOWLEDGMENTS

Our special thanks to Karin Koser of the Georgia Department of Industry, Trade and Tourism and the department's regional representatives: especially Cheryl Smith for the Northeast Mountains, Kitty Sykes for the Colonial Coast, and Becky Bassett for the Presidential Pathways; also Mary Jo Dudley of Plantation Trace and Dawn Townsend for the Northwest Mountains, as well as Jenny Stacy, Savannah Convention and Visitors Bureau.

Thanks to Ernie Wilkins and Truell Myers of Callaway Gardens; Wayne Wilkins of the Franklin D. Roosevelt State Park Stables; Chris Watford of Call of the Wild, and the entire staff of Go With the Flow.

A very special thank-you to Don Starkey of the National Park Service for a private tour of Cumberland Island National Seashore.

Considerable material was provided by the Georgia Department of Natural Resources, Game and Fish Division, Fisheries Section; the National Park Service; the U.S. Army Corps of Engineers; the U.S. Forest Service; and the U.S. Fish and Wildlife Service.

The authors made every attempt to ensure that addresses, telephone numbers, and specific activities listed were correct as of December 15, 1993. However, companies go out of business, move, change their hours, and so forth, so all the information herein is subject to change.

INTRODUCTION

Georgia offers an abundance of outdoor recreational activities, in part because of its moderate climate, its size (it is the largest state east of the Mississippi), and its varied topography—everything from jagged peaks to offshore islands. Any activity that you can do outdoors can probably be done in Georgia—hiking, biking, fishing, camping, horseback riding, sailing, sporting clays, slow and white-water boating, snow skiing, and scuba diving. You can even go llama trekking.

Interest in Georgia's rich sports offerings grows and grows as the 1996 Olympics approach. Venues all over the state will be hosting different official events, and many practice and trial meets will take place at those sites and others. Millions of dollars are being poured into creating and improving sports venues—a boon for residents and visitors alike.

Forests cover about seventy percent of Georgia, providing numerous opportunities to commune with nature.

Beginning in the rugged mountains along the state's northern boundary, Georgia consists of the Appalachian Plateau Region, the Appalachian Ridge and Valley Region, and the Blue Ridge Region. These areas are characterized by peaks and valleys covered with hardwood and pine forests, laurels, and rhododendrons. Turbulent rivers pound down the mountain slopes, begetting roaring waterfalls as they slash through the valleys. More than twenty peaks are higher than 4,000 feet.

The small **Appalachian Plateau Region**, in the northwestern corner of the state, contains wooded peaks as high as 2,000 feet above sea level.

The larger **Appalachian Ridge and Valley Region**, also located in Northwest Georgia, contains broad valleys separated by long, parallel ridges of sandstone rocks.

With peaks that range from 2,000 feet above sea level to the highest summit in the state at almost 5,000 feet, the **Blue Ridge Region** is noted for its spirited white water. Several 1996 Summer Olympics white-water events will take place here.

The three mountainous areas provide challenging opportunities for strenuous hiking, white-water river running, horseback riding, mountain biking, trout fishing, and wilderness camping.

From the mountains, the terrain descends from about 1,500 feet of elevation through a broad region of rolling hills until it finally ends at the Fall Line, where the elevation is only 400 feet. This region, called the **Piedmont**, contains numerous lakes and more gently flowing rivers, although there are a few rapids.

Two coastal plains cover the entire southern part of the state. The **Atlantic Coastal Plain** in the eastern section is relatively flat and characterized by light, sandy soil and slow-moving rivers that empty into the Atlantic Ocean. Scrub pines and live oaks draped with Spanish moss tower over a thick undergrowth of grass, small shrubs, palmettos, and vines. The mysterious Okefenokee Swamp on Georgia's southern border offers activities such as fishing, canoeing, hiking, and primitive camping.

The southwestern part of the state is covered by the **East Coast Coastal Plain**. It is similar to its Atlantic cousin except that its soil is richer and its rivers flow into the Gulf of Mexico.

Georgia has 100 miles of coastline on the Atlantic Ocean. However, if you include all the bays, offshore islands, and river mouths, the coastline would measure 2,344 miles. Twelve barrier islands, collectively known as the Golden Isles, feature miles and miles of unspoiled beaches. Throughout the state, rivers harnessed by hydroelectric power dams create lakes and reservoirs that are used heavily for recreational purposes.

With an average temperature of 65° Georgia enjoys mild weather most of the year. Winter (if you can call it that) is short and mild. With the exception of the occasional rogue storm, only the northern mountains experience snow and very cold temperatures, and then only a few times a year. Despite the dearth of cold weather, Georgia boasts a ski area. The mountain regions are characterized by cool summers, while the remainder of the state is hot and humid. The southern areas are the hottest. Fortunately, the coast and barrier islands are cooled by an ever-present sea breeze.

The **Seven Wonders of Georgia** spotlight some of Georgia's unique features and related recreational activities:

- **Amicalola Falls**, near Dawsonville in the northern mountains, is the state's tallest waterfall, dropping 729 feet.
- **Okefenokee Swamp**, in Southeast Georgia, is 700 square miles of swamp.
- **Providence Canyon**, near Lumpkin in West Central

Georgia, is known as Georgia's Little Grand Canyon. Deep ravines and unusual rock formations have formed in only 100 years of erosion.

• **Radium Springs**, near Albany, is the state's largest natural spring, with a constant temperature of 68° F. Native Americans believed it had magical powers. Swimming is permitted during the summer.

• **Stone Mountain**, near Atlanta, is the world's largest bas-relief sculpture on a granite outcropping. It is carved with a representation of Confederate Civil War heroes Jefferson Davis, Robert E. Lee, and Stonewall Jackson.

• **Tallulah Falls**, in the northeast mountains, flows through a spectacular gorge.

• **Warm Springs**, in West Central Georgia, is a mineral spring reported to have restorative qualities. Still being used for therapy, the waters provided relief for President Franklin D. Roosevelt.

Environmental awareness has caused an upsurge in sports that are kind to our surroundings. Hiking, rock climbing, sailing, rafting, canoeing, and kayaking are all healthy, family recreations that don't consume fuel or injure wildlife.

This guide to outdoor recreational activities in Georgia is designed for natives, newcomers, or visitors to our state. Chapters are devoted to the most common open-air pastimes. We've included activities that you can participate in alone, with your family, or in a small group. We've decided not to include golf, tennis, hunting, purely spectator sports, or team sports such as volleyball.

Each chapter highlights some exceptional opportunities and locations for participating in that sport and then lists some, but by no means all, other options for participating.

Addresses and phone numbers are provided so you can easily get further information. Rates and hours of operation are not included because they change so frequently.

Chapter 10, "Something for Everyone," gives brief descriptions of dozens of other outdoor activities. Before the book even went to press, we were getting suggestions for other activities that we will include in the next edition.

Chapter 11, "Special Places," describes locations in the state that provide multiple recreational opportunities. For example, the Okefenokee Swamp offers wildlife observation, photography, hiking, camping, canoeing, bicycling, fishing, wilderness canoeing/camping, and special events.

Chapter 12, "Organizations and Providers," lists clubs and organizations that span several sports or are sources of general information. Chapter 13 lists visitors and welcome centers by area, lists books and pamphlets you might want to read, and gives sources for maps and other helpful materials.

Every state likes to be the "best" or have the "most" of something. Georgia is no exception. Snaring the 1996 Summer Olympics is a case in point. Sometimes, though, that desire can create confusion. For example, Georgia has 159 counties, more than any other state in America. Unfortunately, the unwieldy number of counties often results in duplication of services and perhaps more than one entity you need to contact for information. To simplify your efforts, the state has created nine tourism regions. You can contact the Georgia Department of Industry, Trade and Tourism for overall state information about a specific region, or you can contact each region directly.

NINE TOURISM REGIONS

Atlanta Metro includes Atlanta, its suburbs, and surrounding counties.

Classic South includes Augusta, Washington, and Waynesboro as well as Lakes Oconee and Clarks Hill.

Colonial Coast includes Savannah, St. Marys, the Golden Isles, and the Okefenokee Swamp.

Historic Heartland includes Macon, Athens, Milledgeville, Eatonton, Madison, and Lakes Oconee, Juliette, and Jackson.

Magnolia Midlands includes Dublin and Statesboro as well as Lake Lindsay Grace.

Northeast Mountains includes many significant towns, just a few of which are Clayton, Clarkesville, Helen, Cleveland, Dahlonega, and Sautee as well as many of the state's most notable white-water rivers and waterfalls.

Northwest Mountains includes Calhoun, Dalton, Rome, and Chickamauga, as well as Cloudland Canyon and several significant white-water rivers.

Plantation Trace in extreme South Georgia is so named because the area between Thomasville, Georgia, and Tallahassee, Florida, contains the largest concentration of working plantations in the country. The region also includes Albany, Tifton, and Valdosta as well as Lakes Seminole, George Andrews, and Walter F. George.

Presidential Pathways gets its name from the two former presidents who called it home. Franklin D. Roosevelt's Little White House was located at Warm Springs, where he sought treatment for polio. Plains is the home of Jimmy Carter.

Area codes can help to orient you. The counties around

Atlanta are represented by the 404 area code. In general, the southern part of the state is represented by 912 and the northern part by 706.

We have not participated in all these sports; in fact, we didn't even know some of them (such as tree climbing) existed. We have taken part in some of these activities and have experienced or visited many of the locations described as well as talked to several of the operators of the activities. But we certainly haven't visited or personally inspected every place mentioned. For additional information, we've relied on recommendations from the state, counties, friends, outfitters, organizations, and other sources.

In addition to the information we've provided here, we suggest contacting a YMCA or YWCA, a parks and recreation department, or a community college near you. They often sponsor classes and outings.

We've included a chapter on camping and several activities that include accommodations. In addition, Georgia boasts a wealth of bed and breakfasts—over 150—that are often the only accommodations in small towns and rural areas. Refer to our book, *Georgia B&Bs* (Country Roads Press, 1994). Another lodging option is a houseboat. On Lake Lanier, you can rent several sizes from Go Vacations, 800-262-3454.

Now that you know what's available, make your plans, get out of your chair, go outside, and discover Georgia's great outdoors.

BICYCLING

We've heard of going head-over-heels for your sport before, but that's not what Carol had in mind. We were mountain biking down a ridge in the National Forest when our group leader stopped to survey the situation. Everyone dutifully halted and waited. As Carol stopped and put one foot down, the whole edge of the path gave way, and, bike and all, she tumbled down the steep slope. Fortunately, it was autumn, and the thick blanket of leaves cushioned her fall. Nothing was bruised but her ego. Lesson learned: on a steep trail with a drop-off, put down the inside foot, not the outside one.

Bicycling is fast becoming America's favorite pastime. This boom started with the increased exposure bicycling received in the early eighties as runners started looking for a less injury prone sport. Participation in biathlons (bike/run) and triathlons (bike/swim/run) increased. Interest also

1

was sparked by the cycling events in the 1984 Los Angeles Olympics.

Georgia's terrain offers a wide variety of biking experiences, from rigorous cycling through spectacular mountains to leisurely touring along the unspoiled coastline and everything in between.

Know before you go: Georgia law recognizes the bicycle as a vehicle, subject to the same rights and responsibilities as a motor vehicle. Bicycles are required to stay as far to the right side of the road as possible and to use side paths or bike lanes where available. Bicycles should travel single file when traffic is present and must never be ridden more than two abreast. No bicycles are permitted on Georgia's Interstate system. When traveling after dark, bicycles must be equipped with a suitable lighting system.

When riding on any road, sidewalk, or bike path, any rider under sixteen must wear a helmet meeting or exceeding the impact standards set by the American National Standards Institute (ANSI) or the Snell Memorial Foundation. Anyone renting a bike to children under sixteen is required to furnish a helmet. Georgia and New Jersey are the only states that have statewide compulsory bicycle helmet legislation.

Several county governments in the Atlanta Regional Commission are planning improvements for cycle use: signed routes; multiuse trails; traffic signals that cyclists can change; parking racks; removal of dangerous grates and other roadway hazards; re-striping of roads to create wide curb lanes, shoulders, or bike lanes; and connections to mass transit.

TOURING

Tourism Division
Georgia Department of Industry, Trade and Tourism

P.O. Box 1776
Atlanta, GA 30301
404-656-3590

By far your best resource about places to bike is a free book-let called "Georgia Bicycle Touring Guide," compiled by the Georgia Tourism Division of the Georgia Department of Industry, Trade and Tourism.

The pocket-size guide includes ten touring routes, com-plete with maps, describing the terrain as well as a few impor-tant attractions and lodging possibilities along the way. The authors made an effort to select lightly traveled roadways. Routes range from 112 miles to 475 miles long; of course, you can tour small portions of any route or combine several routes for a longer trip.

The guide includes addresses and phone numbers for all the state parks and numbers of all the State Patrol Head-quarters, among other helpful numbers. The following con-densation of the routes described by the guide is used with the permission of the Department of Industry, Trade and Tourism.

The **Mountain Crossing** route (120 miles generally east-west) is the most scenic, but also the most difficult. It drops and climbs over and over from Lookout Mountain on the ex-treme northwestern border of the state to Black Rock State Park in the extreme northeastern part of the state. Important attractions along the way include Cloudland Canyon and Fort Mountain State Parks, Amicalola Falls, Dahlonega (site of the nation's first gold rush), Vogel and Unicoi State Parks, the alpine village of Helen, Lakes Burton and Rabun, and Tallulah Falls.

The **Chattahoochee Trace** route (352 miles north-south) begins at Cloudland Canyon in the northwest and traces a route along the western part of the state past James H. "Sloppy" Floyd and Tanner State Parks and continues through the Presidential Pathways region, where you can explore Pine Mountain, Warm Springs, Franklin D. Roosevelt State Park, Roosevelt's Little White House, and Callaway Gardens. Farther south, you can visit the National Infantry Museum at Fort Benning. The area around Lumpkin contains several must-see attractions. In town, visit the Bedingfield Inn (a museum), a turn-of-the-century pharmacy, and an old general store. Westville, a living-history village, is located nearby. Providence Canyon is known as Georgia's Little Grand Canyon. The route continues past Florence Marina State Park on Lake Walter F. George, a Frontier Village in Fort Gaines, the Kolomoki Indian Mounds State Historic Park, Coheelee Creek Covered Bridge, and Lake Seminole.

The **Trans-Georgia** route (232 miles west-east) winds through gently rolling sand hills in middle Georgia, where elevations are generally less than 750 feet. It begins in historic Columbus on the Georgia/Alabama border, continues through Junction City—home of the state's largest sand mines—and past numerous peach orchards. Take a short side trip to visit the Air Museum at Robins Air Force Base. You'll ride through several small Southern towns, past George L. Smith State Park, and finish the trip in Savannah.

The **Savannah River Run** route (272 miles north-south) takes you from the foothills of the Piedmont Plateau in the northeastern corner of the state to the Atlantic Ocean at Savannah. The change in elevation is 700 feet. Attractions along the way include Toccoa Falls, and Lakes Hartwell, Richard B. Russell, and Clarks Hill. The historic towns of Washington and Augusta make good side trips.

The **Coastal** route (112 miles north-south) affords an opportunity to experience the coast and barrier islands of

Georgia. Points of interest along the way include Savannah, Skidaway Island, Richmond Hill, and Crooked River State Parks, as well as Fort King George and the charming towns of Darien and St. Marys. Worthwhile side trips include Skidaway, Wilmington, Tybee, St. Simons, Sea, Jekyll, and Cumberland Islands.

Southern Crossing (208 miles east-west) is a relatively easy ride across Southern Georgia. The outstanding highlight of this route is the Okefenokee Swamp. You can enter the park at Folkston, Fargo, or Waycross. Thomasville, the Rose City, is the home of the Rose Test Garden (operated by the Thomasville Nursery) and has several historic districts to explore. The area between Thomasville and Tallahassee, Florida, contains the largest concentration of working plantations in the country. Pebble Hill Plantation is open to the public for tours. Also visit Seminole, Adele Reed Bingham, Kolomoki Mounds, Okefenokee Swamp, Laura S. Walker, and Jekyll Island State Parks.

The **Wiregrass Route** (176 miles east-west) is relatively flat with occasional rolling hills. Begin at the Kolomoki Mounds State Park in the southwestern corner of the state, stop off at Albany to visit the zoo at Chehaw Park, then tarry in Tifton to visit the Agrirama, a living-history museum. The trail ends near Laura S. Walker State Park and the Okefenokee Swamp.

The **Atlanta Link** (120 miles north-south) from Helen in Northeast Georgia provides a downhill ride through rolling terrain to Atlanta. The best way to see the city is to lock up your bike somewhere and tour the city on MARTA (Metropolitan Atlanta Rapid Transit Authority), a system of buses and trains. Bikes are not permitted on buses but are permitted on the last car of rail trains all day on weekends and weekdays except from 6:00 A.M. to 9:00 A.M. and 3:30 P.M. to

6:30 P.M. The trail continues south to the Pine Mountain/ Warm Springs area.

Follow Sherman's mountainous march from Fort Ogle- thorpe in Northwest Georgia to Atlanta on the **Central Route** (368 miles north-south) and then on through flattened terrain clear to the southern border of the state. You'll pass High Falls, Indian Springs, Red Top Mountain, and Georgia Veterans State Parks and Lake Tobesofkee.

The three-part **March to the Sea** route (475 miles north- west-southeast) traces the infamous Civil War route of Sher- man's army from Atlanta to Savannah.

Part 1, the **Atlanta Campaign**, stretches 100 miles from Chickamauga National Battlefield Park in Fort Oglethorpe to Kennesaw National Battlefield Park in Marietta, an Atlanta suburb.

Part 2, **Siege of Atlanta**, extends forty-seven miles through the capital city to Stone Mountain Park.

Part 3, **March to the Sea**, follows the course taken by Sherman's left flank from Stone Mountain to Savannah—300 miles. This section includes antebellum towns spared by the army as well as Hard Labor Creek, Richmond Hill, and Skida- way Island State Parks.

Augusta Canal Authority
801 Broad Street, Room 507
Augusta, GA 30901
706-722-1071

The nine-mile **Augusta Canal** is a National Historic Land- mark. Today, just as when it opened in 1846, the canal pro- vides industrial and recreational uses. The canal is being restored and refurbished so that it and the landmark buildings along it will be preserved.

The old towpath, where mules towed the barges up and down the canal, is an excellent bike route. It follows the entire length either along the inland side or along the land separation between the canal and the Savannah River.

A levee, separate from the canal bank, runs seven miles along the canal. Part of it is incorporated into the Riverwalk Park and offers easy riding. You can also cycle around Lakes Warren and Olmstead, which are connected to the canal.

The distance from the dam to I-20 is 2.05 miles, from the dam to the pumping station 3.5 miles, from the dam to 13th Street 7 miles, and from the dam to Riverwalk 8.5 miles.

In 1773, naturalist William Bartram explored along the Savannah River. You can see many of the same plants and animals that he recorded.

Bicycle Ride Across Georgia
P.O. Box 576
Stone Mountain, GA 30086-0576
404-279-9797

Participants in the 1993 **Bicycle Ride Across Georgia** (the fourteenth) pedaled 424 miles from Atlanta to Savannah, averaging 60 miles per day. The 1994 trip will cover 400 miles, from Bainbridge in Southwest Georgia to St. Simons Island off the Georgia Coast.

BRAG is a family-oriented tour, not a race. The purpose is recreational, social, and educational. Approximately 2,500 people from all over the country participate in this yearly event. Proceeds are donated to charity.

Routed through lightly traveled back roads, the tour is an excellent way to see the state at a quiet, unhurried pace. Participants travel at their own tempo and meet at the end of each day. You can choose to camp or stay in a motel. During the afternoon and evening, activities and entertainment are planned. People are responsible for their own meals, but at frequent rest stops, water and refreshments are provided. The affair culminates in an End-of-the-Road Party.

Vehicles are not permitted on the tour route. Many family members in private vehicles travel alternate routes, inter-secting with the bike route at frequent intervals. All private vehicles must be registered and must display a BRAG parking permit.

Support vehicles travel the route with water and limited first-aid supplies. Baggage trucks provide daily transportation for camping and personal gear. The amount and size of bag-gage is restricted. Riders are responsible for loading their own gear. Repair service is provided at a nominal cost. Buses bring riders, cycles, and gear back to the starting point.

Callaway Gardens Resort
P.O. Box 2000
Pine Mountain, GA 31822
800-282-8181

The Discovery Bicycle Trail offers 7.5 miles of leisurely tour-ing through the garden's natural areas. The trail begins at the Bike Barn near the beach parking lot at Robin Lake, where you can rent bikes and helmets if you haven't brought your own. Some bikes are equipped with child safety seats.

The trail meanders past the Day Butterfly Center, the Log Cabin, the Ida Cason Callaway Memorial Chapel, Mr. Cason's Vegetable Garden, and the Sibley Horticultural Center as well as through wooded areas and by streams and lakes. Callaway Gardens boasts one of the largest collections of different vari-eties of azaleas in the country—including the prunifolia, found only within a 100-mile radius. A ferry near the end of the trail at the boat dock transports riders across Mountain Creek Lake and back to the starting point.

COASTAL BIKING

Georgia's wide, flat, hard-packed beaches are ideal for beach riding. The barrier islands offer opportunities for biking on the beach as well as on the interior roads.

A bike lane follows the highway from Brunswick on the mainland to St. Simons Island. On St. Simons, bike trails run for several miles along Frederica Road, Demere Road, Kings Way, and other streets at the southern end of the island.

Jekyll Island State Park features a long bicycle loop trail. In addition, paved bike paths meander through woods and along the beach and marsh for 20 miles of biking/jogging opportunities.

A bike is the only mode of transportation besides walking on the dirt roads and beaches of **Cumberland Island**. However, bicycles aren't allowed on the ferry, so you'll have to make arrangements to get your bike there by private boat.

There are bike trails at Harris Neck, Savannah, and Okefenokee National Wildlife Refuges.

MOUNTAIN BIKING

Mountain biking is the growth sport of the nineties. A few years ago, local riders had to travel to the mid-Atlantic states to find races. Now there are so many races nearby, riders have to choose from among several in a single weekend.

To upgrade your bike for mountain biking, you need to make some changes in your equipment. Most manufacturers

Georgia Outdoor Activity Guide

offer models in the $400 to $800 range, but you can outfit your present bike for much less. Change your original tires to ones that are more condition-specific. The improvements in tire technology will dramatically improve your performance. For example, handlebar extensions, or bar ends, result in better climbing leverage and additional hand positions for greater comfort. Both seated and out-of-the-saddle climbing techniques improve.

Three areas that offer mountain biking trails are the following:

Toccoa Ranger District
Chattahoochee National Forest
Suite 5, Owenby Building
East Main Street
Blue Ridge, GA 30513
706-632-3031

Located in the Toccoa Ranger District, Chattahoochee National Forest, **Rich Mountain Trail** offers a strenuous 8.8-mile single-track experience with elevations ranging from 1,720 feet to 3,400 feet.

The trail begins at Stanley Gap, about thirty minutes from Blue Ridge on the north side of Rock Creek Road. At Deep Gap, cyclists have the option of returning to the beginning spot by a more gentle grade. This shorter route is 5.5 miles. Biking time to complete the entire trail is one to two hours. A proposed hiking/biking trail will include several loops off the main trail.

Warning from the Forest Service: near the top of Rocky Mountain, the trail goes around the east side with steep drop-offs. Extreme caution is demanded. The trail is not suitable for beginners and should be attempted only by experienced

10

off-road bicyclists. When in doubt about your skill level, walk your bike.

If you are not familiar with the North Georgia mountains around Blue Ridge, the directions to the trailhead may be difficult. You'll turn off of Georgia Highway 515 onto County Road 150, right onto County Road 152, right under the overpass, and follow the road an additional 3.2 miles after it becomes dirt and gravel. The total distance is about twelve miles from Blue Ridge, but it takes thirty minutes. Contact the Toccoa Ranger District for more explicit directions.

Cohutta Wilderness
Cohutta Ranger District
Chattahoochee National Forest
401 Old Ellijay Road
Chatsworth, GA 30705
706-695-6736

This rugged portion of the Chattahoochee National Forest is an extremely popular challenge for experienced riders. **Windy Gap Cycle Trail** offers 5 miles of adventure.

Metro Atlanta
Chattahoochee National Recreation Area
National Park Service
1978 Island Ford Parkway
Dunwoody, GA 30350
404-394-7912 or 394-8335 or 952-4419

People don't automatically think of urban Atlanta and mountain biking in the same breath. However, the **Chattahoochee National Recreation Area** offers some good practice/conditioning trails spread along 48 miles of river. Most trails have signs indicating where mountain biking is permitted. While the park is spread out over 48 miles, it is not continuous. What we would probably call branches, the Forest Service calls units.

INSTRUCTION

Dick Lane Velodrome
Sumner Park off Norman Berry Drive
East Point, GA 30344
404-765-1085 or 765-1075

The only velodrome in the Southeast, the City of East Point facility features up to 34-degree banked curves for high-speed bicycle racing for one-speed track bikes. On the concrete outdoor track, cyclists can reach speeds of 40 mph. Classes include bike-handling skills and bike safety, as well as racing tips. Bicycles are supplied for lessons. The annual Georgia Championships are held at the velodrome.

The velodrome is open from March to Labor Day, from 8:00 A.M. to dark. Admission is free. June through August, there are races every Friday night. Race participants must be certified by the American Bicycling Association. Training for several Olympic biking events will be held here in 1996.

OUTFITTERS/RENTALS

Benjy's Bike Shop (rentals)
238 Retreat Village
St. Simons, GA 31522
912-638-6766

Barry's Beach Service
(beach cruisers and BMX)
King & Prince Hotel
St. Simons, GA 31522
912-638-8053
also
Villas by the Sea
and **Holiday Inn**
Jekyll Island, GA 31520
912-638-8053

Cedar Creek
Bicycle Rentals
Cave Spring, GA 30124
404-777-3607 or 777-3586

Eddie Collins
Island Bike Shop (rentals)
204 Sylvan Drive
St. Simons, GA 31522
912-638-0705

Ocean Motion (rentals)
1300 Ocean Boulevard
St. Simons, GA 31522
912-638-5225

Roswell Bicycles
(event sponsor; rentals)
670 Houze Way
Roswell, GA 30075
404-642-4057

CLUBS AND ORGANIZATIONS

Southern Bicycle League, Inc.
P.O. Box 1360
Roswell, GA 30077
404-594-8350

The SBL is a volunteer organization devoted to promoting bicycle riding for recreation as well as basic transportation, protecting bicyclists' rights to the road, educating bicyclists and nonbicyclists regarding safe riding habits, and promoting safe bicycling facilities.

The club sponsors day rides and several annual tours, most of which are overnighters. These tours include Pine Mountain and Callaway Gardens, a Georgia Wine Tour,

Thomasville Rose Pedal, Helen, and several out-of-state expeditions.

Effective cycling courses for the new rider are held with certified instructors. Special "New Rider" events are held regularly. The club holds monthly meetings covering topics such as flat tires, mountain biking, laying out a tour, muscle massage, and commuting. Frequent swap meets are held. Annual events include a summer picnic and a Christmas party.

The club's monthly magazine, *FreeWheelin*, contains an extensive ride calendar and articles on advocacy efforts, safety, health, and ride reports. An added benefit to league members is a 10 percent discount on accessories at many bicycle shops. Individual and family memberships are available.

Condor Cycling Club
2892 Aspen Woods Entry
Doraville, GA 30360
404-416-7231 or 404-427-4430

Affiliated with the United States Cycling Federation, the Condor Cycling Club holds relaxed family recreational rides on Sunday afternoons. Helmets are required. Support vehicles follow with water and refreshments.

Southern Off-Road Bicycle Association
P.O. Box 1191
Decatur, GA 30031
404-876-0943
Contact: David Mayne

SORBA sponsors recreational rides and tours open to riders fourteen years of age and older. Ride leaders are volunteers.

The club meets monthly. Membership includes a monthly newsletter that lists these events as well as competitions and rides for charity sponsored by other organizations.

Augusta Freewheelers
759 Seven Lakes Boulevard
Martinez, GA 30907

Bicycle Club of Atlanta
P.O. Box 12341
Atlanta, GA 30355

**Bicycle Association
of North Georgia**
6085 Valley Stream Drive
Cumming, GA 30103

BRAG (see "Touring," page 7)

**Chattahoochee
Cycling Club**
P.O. Box 4742
Columbus, GA 31904

**Coastal Bicycle
Touring Club**
1326 Grace Drive
Savannah, GA 31406

**Emerald City
Freewheelers**
216 Waverly Drive
Dublin, GA 31201

Gwinnett Touring Club
P.O. Box 464365
Lawrenceville, GA 30246
404-972-8874

Middle Georgia Bike Club
3268 Willowdale Drive
Macon, GA 31204

North Atlanta Road Club
P.O. Box 1243
Decatur, GA 30031

Pecan City Pedalers
3713 Trumpington Lane
Albany, GA 31707

Road Wolves Cycling Club
10687 Alpharetta Highway
Roswell, GA 30075

Statesboro Bicycle Club
P.O. Box 2713
Statesboro, GA 30458

**Vidalia-Toombs
Bicycle Association**
604 Bay Street
Vidalia, GA 30478

Women's Mountain Bike and Tea Society (WOMBATS)
673 East Paces Ferry Road
Atlanta, GA 30303
Contact: Anne Ledbetter

The organization sponsors bike swaps, rides, thrift-shop treasure hunts, tea parties, and other activities. The national organizaton can be contacted at:

WOMBATS
P.O. Box 757
Fairfax, CA 94978
415-459-0980

Other organizations include **Atlanta Bicycle Campaign, Bicycle Federation of Georgia, Central Georgia Cyclists, Coosa Valley Bicycle Association, Covington Cycling Club,** and **Southern Cyclists**.

OTHER SOURCES OF INFORMATION

Georgia Department of Transportation (County maps)
Map Sales Division
2 Capitol Square
Atlanta, GA 30334
404-656-5336

SPECIAL EVENTS

Various organizations sponsor more than 1,000 annual events. Here are just a few.

BRAG (see "Touring," page 7)

Challenge of the Centuries
P.O. Box 433
Hartwell, GA 30643
706-376-6584, ext. 228

The "challenge" is a fun family ride sponsored by the Hartwell Kiwanis Club and corporate sponsors, featuring 35-mile, 100-kilometer, and 100-mile loop rides. Participants may ride one or both days. Routes vary in difficulty from moderate to strenuous. Proceeds from the entry fee are donated to Kiwanis-sponsored youth groups. An ANSI-approved helmet is required. Camping, showers, changing rooms, and rest rooms are available.

Hell of the North/Roswell Bicycles
670 Houze Way
Roswell, GA 30075
404-642-4057

The shop sponsors this ride, considered to be the most challenging road event in the state. Open to anyone, the ride is held four times a year. The route covers 54 miles with 30- and 70-mile options through mostly rural roads of Cherokee and North Fulton counties. Riders will encounter some very steep inclines and lots of broken pavement. Always held on a weekend, the event attracts fifty to 200 riders.

**MS 150 Bike Tour/Georgia Chapter
of the National Multiple Sclerosis Society**
1100 Circle 75 Parkway, Suite 630
Atlanta, GA 30339
404-984-9080 or 800-822-3379

Sponsored by the Georgia Chapter of the National Multiple Sclerosis Society and corporate sponsors, the tour is a two-day, 150-mile cycling challenge pedaling to an overnight location. Riders can choose to camp, bunk in a cabin, or be transported to a local hotel. The tour includes frequent rest stops. Bike mechanics, medical teams, SAG wagons, and communication vehicles accompany the tour. Participants pay a registration fee and obtain a minimum amount of pledges.

Tour D'Town/American Cancer Society
2200 Lake Boulevard, Suite A
Atlanta, GA 30319

Four courses range in distance from 6 to 48 miles. There is a team challenge. Proceeds from the entry fee and pledges are donated to the American Cancer Society. Participants are eligible to win prizes for pledges.

Biking Newsletter

CYCLESouth (newspaper)
1000 St. Charles Avenue, N.E./#4
Atlanta, GA 30306
404-873-1515

2 CAMPING

We woke up one chilly morning to find that we—and our sleeping bags—had slid about five feet down the mountain. The same thing had happened to most of our fellow campers. We were all bivouacked atop Pine Mountain, and only a lucky few had found a patch of level earth to sleep on. Straw was spread on the ground to mask protruding rocks. Much to our chagrin, we learned that tarps and straw just don't mix; they only create a sliding board effect. Apparently every time we turned over in the night, we slid a little farther down the hill. After we all scrambled back up the slope, we had a good laugh about it. It was only later that our creaky old bodies told us we couldn't take too much of the Spartan life.

People's conceptions about what constitutes camping vary considerably. Our idea of camping is staying in a large recreational vehicle with modern conveniences—although we definitely enjoy a respite from the telephone, TV, and VCR. Another person's notion of camping might be sleeping under the stars with nothing but a sleeping bag for creature comfort. Opinions about camping can run the gamut between these two extremes.

Georgia offers an abundance of camping experiences— not only from the standpoint of physical comfort, but also in terms of location. You can pitch your tent or park your RV anywhere from the ocean's edge to the highest mountain peak.

STATE PARKS AND HISTORIC SITES

Georgia State Parks and Historic Sites
1352 Floyd Tower East
205 Butler Street, S.E.
Atlanta, GA 30334
404-656-3530
800-3GA-PARK in Georgia
800-5GA-PARK outside Georgia

Georgia's thirty-nine state park campgrounds offer a variety of camping experiences, including tent or trailer camping, RV sites, backpack camping, pioneer camping, and group camping.

At the state parks, tent/RV/trailer campsites feature electrical and water hookups, cooking grills, and picnic tables. Most sites are available on a first-come, first-served basis, although each campground has a few sites that can be reserved in advance. A small camping fee is charged. Occupancy of the same site is limited to fourteen days.

Pioneer campsites have water and primitive sanitary facilities. A small charge per person is charged, and advance

20

reservations are required. Several parks have group camping facilities and lodges. Many include sleeping quarters, kitchen, dining/assembly room, activity areas, and swimming areas. Rental rates vary, and reservations are required.

All campgrounds have modern comfort stations and dump sites, and many have laundry facilities and a camp store. Outdoor activities at most state parks include bicycling, hiking, fishing, boating, and swimming. Several parks offer golf and tennis, miniature golf, pedal boats, and even horseback riding.

U.S. ARMY CORPS OF ENGINEERS LAKES

U.S. Army Corps of Engineers
30 Pryor Street, S.W.
Atlanta, GA 30335-6801
404-331-6715
Lake Allatoona 404-688-7870 or 404-974-9476
Lake Lanier 404-945-9531 or 404-945-1466

Georgia is blessed with an abundance of lakes, many of which were created and are maintained by the U.S. Army Corps of Engineers. The lakes include Allatoona, Carters, Clarks Hill, Hartwell, Richard B. Russell, Sidney Lanier, Walter F. George, George W. Andrews, and West Point. The Corps maintains many campsites at these lakes—all with full hookups, dump stations, and shower houses. Some have boat access and washers and dryers.

At most of the campgrounds, a fee is charged for developed camping sites. Visitors to campers are also charged a fee. There are no fees for day-use areas.

21

ACCOMMODATIONS AND ACTIVITIES

The **Accommodations and Activities** chart indicates the address, phone number, and location of Georgia's state parks and historic sites, as well as overnight accommodations and recreational activities.

STATE PARKS	ADDRESS, ZIP & TELEPHONE	LOCATION	Tent & Trailer Sites	Lodge	Cottages	Group Camp/Lodge - Yes (Y) No (N)	Picnic Sites	Picnic Shelters	Group Shelters	Lake	Boating Ramp (R) Dock (D) Private Boats Allowed (P) Limits on Motors (L) Waterskiing (W)	Boats for Rent - Fishing (F) Canoe (C) Pedal (P)	Fishing - Lake (L) Stream (S)	Swimming - Pool (P) Beach (B)	Golf (G) Tennis (T)	Trails - Nature (N) Hiking (H)	Museum or Exhibits	Near Interstate (10 mi. or less)
A. H. Stephens Historic Park	P.O. Box 235, Crawfordville. 30631; (706) 456-2602	2 mi. N of I-20 in Crawfordville	25			Y/N	50	1		*	PL	F	L				*	*
Amicalola Falls Park and Lodge	Star Route. Box 215. Dawsonville. 30534. (706) 265-8888	16 mi. N.W. of Dawsonville via Ga. 183 & 52	17	57 rms	14		78	5					S			NH	*	
Black Rock Mountain Park	Mountain City. 30562. (706) 746-2141	3 mi. N of Clayton via U.S. 441	53		10		38	2					L			NH	*	
Bobby Brown Park	Route 4. Box 232. Elberton. 30635. (706) 213-2046	21 mi. S.E. of Elberton off Ga. 72	61				40	3	1	*	RDPW		L	P		N		
Cloudland Canyon Park	Route 2. Box 150. Rising Fawn. 30738. (706) 657-4050	25 mi. N.W. of Lafayette off Ga. 136	75		16	N/Y	123	4	1				L	P		H		*
Crooked River Park	3092 Spur 40. St. Mary s. 31558. (912) 882-5256	7 mi. N of St. Mary's on Ga. Spur 40	60		11		75	5	1	*	RDPW		S	P	T	N		*
Elijah Clark Park	Route 4. Box 293. Lincolnton. 30817. (706) 359-3458	7 mi. SE of Lincolnton off U.S. 378	165		20		121	5	1	*	RPW		L	B		N	*	*
F.D. Roosevelt Park	2970 Ga. Hwy. 190. Pine Mountain. 31822. (706) 663-4858	5 mi. S.E of Pine Mtn. on Ga. 190	140		21	Y/N	120	6	1	*	D	F	L	PB		NH	*	
Florence Marina Park	Route 1. Box 36. Omaha. 31821. (912) 838-6870	16 mi. W of Lumpkin at end of Ga. 39 C	44		10		25	1	1	*	RDPW	F	L	P	T	N	*	*
Ft. McAllister Historic Park	Box 394-A. Richmond Hill. 31324. (912) 727-2339	10 mi. E. of I-95 and U.S. 17 on Spur 144	65				50	2	1	*	RDPW		S			N	*	*
Ft. Mountain Park	Route 7. Box 7008. Chatsworth. 30705. (706) 695-2621	7 mi. E of Chatsworth via Ga. 52	70		15		117	7	1	*		P	L	B		NH	*	*
Ft. Yargo Park and Will-A-Way Recreation Area	P.O. Box 764. Winder. 30680. (404) 867-3489 / (404) 867-5313	1 mi. S. of Winder on Ga. 81	47	30 rms	3	Y/N	75 / 10	5	2	*	RDPL	FCP	L	B	T	N		
General Coffee Park	Route 2. Box 83. Nicholls. 31554. (912) 384-7082	6 mi. E of Douglas on Hwy. 32	25		10		60	6	1	*	RDPW		L	P		N		
George L. Smith Park	P.O. Box 57. Twin City. 30471. (912) 763-2759	4 mi. S.E of Twin City off Ga. Hwy. 23	21				50	4	1	*	RDPL	FC	LS		G	NH		
George T. Bagby Park/Lake Walter F. George Lodge	Route 1. Box 201. Ft. Gaines. 31751. (912) 768-2571	4 mi. N of Fort Gaines off Hwy. 39		30 rms	5		50	1		*	RDPW	FCP	LS	B	GT	N	*	
Georgia Veterans Park	2459-A U S Hwy. 280 W. Cordele. 31015. (912) 276-2371	9 mi. W of Cordele via U.S. 2	83		10		50	3	2	*	RDPW		L	B P	T		*	*
Gordonia-Alatamaha Park	P.O. Box 1047. Reidsville. 30453. (912) 557-6444	City limits of Reidsville off U.S. 280	23				50	4	1	*			L	PB	G			
Hamburg Park	Route 1. Box 233. Mitchell. 30820. (912) 552-2393	16 mi. N.E. of Sandersville on Hamburg Rd	30			Y/N	60	2	1	*	FP	FP	L	P	GT			
Hard Labor Creek Park	P.O. Box 247. Rutledge. 30663. (706) 557-2863	2 mi. N. of Rutledge off U.S. 278	49		20	Y/N	50	5	2	*	RPL	FCP	LS	B	G	NH	*	
Hart Park	1515 Hart Park Rd. Hartwell. 30643. (706) 376-8756	3 mi. N of Hartwell off U.S. 29	65		2		85	3		*	RDPW		L	B		NH		
High Falls Park	Route 5. Box 202-A. Jackson. 30233. (912) 994-5080	10 mi. N. of Forsyth off I-75 exit #65	142				50	5	1	*	RPL		L	PB	G	N	*	
Indian Springs Park	Route 1. Box 439. Flovilla. 30216. (404) 775-7241	5 mi. S of Jackson on Hwy. 42	90		10	Y/N	3	7	1	*	RDPL	FP	LS	P		N	*	
James H. "Sloppy" Floyd Park	Route 1. Box 291. Summerville. 30747. (706) 857-5211	3 mi. S.E of Summerville off U.S. 27	25				94	2	1	*	RDPL	FP	L	B		NH	*	
John Tanner Park	354 Tanner's Beach Rd. Carrollton. 30117. (404) 830-2222	6 mi. W of Carrollton on Ga. 16	78		6	N/Y	20	4	2	*	PL	FCP	L	B		N		
Kolomoki Mounds Historic Park	Route 1. Box 114. Blakely. 31723. (912) 723-5296	6 mi. N of Blakely off U.S. 27	35			Y/N	71	7	2	*	RDPL	F	LS	P		N	*	
Laura S. Walker Park	5653 Laura Walker Rd.. Waycross. 31501. (912) 287-4900	10 mi. S.E. of Waycross on Ga. 177	44			Y/N	250	9	4	*	RDPLW	C	L	P		N		

Name	Address, ZIP & Telephone	Location															
Little Ocmulgee Park/ Pete Phillips Lodge	P.O. Box 149, McRae, 31055, (912) 868-7474	2 mi. N. of McRae off Hwy. 441	58	30 rms.	10	Y/N	91	6	1	*	RDPLW	FC	L			NH	
Magnolia Springs Park	Route 5, Box 488, Millen, 30442, (912) 982-1660	5 mi. N. of Millen on U.S. 25	26		5	Y/N	150	8	3	*	RDPLW	FC	L	P		NH	*
Mistletoe Park	Route 1, Box 335, Appling, 30802, (706) 541-0321	12 mi. N. of I-20 at exit #60	107		10		25	4	1	*	RDPW		L	B		NH	*
Moccasin Creek Park	Route 1, Box 1634, Clarkesville, 30523, (706) 947-3194	20 mi. N. of Clarkesville on Ga. 197	53				6	1		*	RDPW		LS			NH	*
Panola Mountain Conservation Park	2600 Highway 155, S.W., Stockbridge, 30281, (404) 389-7801	18 mi. S.E. of Atlanta on Ga. Hwy. 155					25	4								NH	* *
Providence Canyon Conservation Park	Route 1, Box 158, Lumpkin, 31815, (912) 838-6202	7 mi. W. of Lumpkin on Ga. 39C	125		18		65	2								NH	* *
Red Top Mountain Park and Lodge	653 Red Top Mountain Rd., S.E., Cartersville, 30120, (404) 975-0055	1½ mi. E. of I-75 exit #123		33 rms.		18	50	7	2	*	RDPW		L	B	T	NH	* *
Reed Bingham Park	Route 2, Box 394 B-1, Adel, 31620, (912) 896-3551	6 mi. W. of Adel on Ga. 37 via I-75 exit #10	85				74	7	4	*	DPW		LS	B		N	
Richard B. Russell Park	Route 2, Box 118, Elberton, 30635, (706) 213-2045	10 mi. N. of Elberton off Ga. 77 on Ruckersville Rd.					40	3		*	RDPW		L	B		N	
Seminole Park	Route 2, Donalsonville, 31745, (912) 861-3137	16 mi. S. of Donalsonville via Ga. 39	50		10		100	6	1	*	RDPW	F	L	B		N	*
Skidaway Island Park	Diamond Causeway, Savannah, 31406, (912) 598-2300	6 mi. S.E. of Savannah off Diamond Causeway	88				100	5	1	*	RPW		S	P		NH	*
S. C. Foster Park	Route 1, Box 131, Fargo, 31631, (912) 637-5274	18 mi. N.E. of Fargo via Ga. 177	66		9		20	3		*	RDPL	FC	L			N	*
Sweetwater Creek Conservation Park	P.O. Box 816, Lithia Springs, 30057, (404) 944-1700	15 mi. W. of Atlanta off I-20 exit #12					48	11	1	*	RDPL	FC	LS			NH	*
Tugaloo Park	Route 1, Box 1766, Lavonia, 30553, (706) 356-4362	6 mi. N. of Lavonia off Ga. Hwy. 328	120		20		100	7	1	*	RDPW	P	L	B	T	NH	*
Unicoi Park and Lodge	P.O. Box 849, Helen, 30545, (706) 878-2824	2 mi. N. of Helen on Hwy. 356	84	100 rms.	30	Y/N	70	6	1	*		CP	LS	B	T	NH	*
Victoria Bryant Park	Route 1, Box 1767, Royston, 30662, (706) 245-6270	4 mi. W. of Royston off U.S. 29	25				97	5		*			LS	P	G	NH	*
Vogel Park	Route 1, Box 1230, Blairsville, 30512, (706) 745-2628	11 mi. S. of Blairsville via U.S. Hwy. 19/129	110		36		65	4	1	*		P	LS	B		NH	*
Watson Mill Bridge Park	Route 1, Box 190, Comer, 30629, (706) 783-5349	6 mi. S. of Comer on Ga. 22	21				70	3		*	P	FCP	LS	B		NH	*
STATE HISTORIC SITES	ADDRESS, ZIP & TELEPHONE	LOCATION															
Dahlonega Gold Museum	Public Square, Box 2042, Dahlonega, 30533, (706) 864-2257	Public Square in Dahlonega															*
Etowah Indian Mounds	813 Indian Mounds Rd., S.W., Cartersville, 30120, (404) 387-3747	5.5 mi. S.W. of I-75 off Ga. 61					7									N	* *
Fort King George	P.O. Box 711, Darien, 31305, (912) 437-4770	3 mi. E. of I-95 in Darien at exit #10					7									N	* *
Fort Morris	Route 1, Box 236, Midway, 31320, (912) 884-5999	7 mi. E. of I-95 exit #13					7									N	* *
Hofwyl-Broadfield Plantation	Route 10, Box 83, Brunswick, 31520, (912) 264-9263	Between Brunswick & Darien, 1 mi. E. of I-95 exit #9					1									N	* *
Jarrell Plantation	Route 2, Box 220, Juliette, 31046, (912) 986-5172	18 mi. E. of I-75 at exit #60 off Ga. 18					4									N	* *
Lapham-Patterson House	626 N. Dawson St., Thomasville, 31792, (912) 225-4004	626 N. Dawson St., Thomasville					1										*
Little White House	Rt. 1, Box 10, Warm Springs, 31830, (706) 655-3511	½ mi. S. of Warm Springs on Ga. 85W					25										*
New Echota Cherokee Capital	1211 Chatsworth Hwy., N.E., Calhoun, 30701, (706) 629-9151	1 mi. E. of I-75 exit #131 via Ga. 225							1								* *
Pickett's Mill Battlefield	2640 Mt. Tabor Rd., Dallas, 30132, (404) 443-7850	5 mi. N.E. of Dallas															* *
Robert Toombs House	P.O. Box 605, Washington, 30673, (706) 678-2226	City limits of Washington					2									NH	*
Traveler's Rest	Route 3, Toccoa, 30577, (706) 886-2256	7 mi. E. of Toccoa off U.S. 123															*
Chief Vann House	Route 7, Box 7655, Chatsworth, 30705, (706) 695-2598	At intersection of Ga. 52 & Ga. 225					2										* *
Wormsloe	7601 Skidaway Rd., Savannah, 31406, (912) 353-3023	8 mi. S.E. of Savannah via Skidaway Rd.					5									N	* *

(Reproduced with permission of Georgia Department of Parks and Natural Resources.)

GEORGIA POWER COMPANY LAKES

Georgia Power Company Land Development Field Offices:
    Chattahoochee River, 404-329-1455
    Lake Oconee/Lake Sinclair, 404-526-3663
    Lake Jackson, 404-526-2741
    North Georgia Lakes, 404-526-3978
    Bartlett's Ferry, 404-526-4305

The state's electric utility maintains several lakes for hydroelectric power generation: Lakes Sinclair and Oconee on the Oconee River, Lake Jackson on the Ocmulgee River, and Lake Harding on the Chattahoochee River. Georgia Power has developed several recreational areas to give the public access to the lakes. All have day-use facilities, some offer camping facilities. Most of these recreation areas offer water sports, boat ramps, picnicking, and playgrounds. Fees are charged for day use and camping.

The public-use areas that offer camping have campsites with water and electrical hookups, picnic tables, and grills. There are also tent sites with picnic tables and grills. Each campground offers a comfort station with hot showers, washers and dryers, soft drink machines, ice, a pay telephone, and a central dump station. Wilderness camping areas are available for groups.

These lakes have other public-use areas that are managed by the Georgia Department of Natural Resources, the U.S. Forest Service, or some other entity.

CHATTAHOOCHEE-OCONEE NATIONAL FORESTS

U.S. Forest Service
508 Oak Street N.W.

Gainesville, GA 30501
404-536-0541

Georgia has two National Forests—the Chattahoochee, with 749,444 acres in the mountains of North Georgia; and the Oconee, with 109,268 acres in the rolling Piedmont of middle Georgia. The two forests offer three wilderness areas, as well as the Chattooga Wild and Scenic River, six swimming beaches, thousands of acres of lakes and streams, and over 300 miles of trails. In addition, the national forests contain over 500 developed campsites.

Most of the developed recreation areas are open from late spring to early fall. However, a few areas accommodate winter campers.

Primitive camping is allowed anywhere in the national forests unless posted otherwise. For example, camping is not permitted in picnicking or swimming sites and scenic spots. Permits are not needed for camping or for a campfire.

Trailers and motor homes (those less than twenty-two feet long) are permitted in the general forest area and in the developed recreation sites. No water or electrical hookups are provided.

You cannot reserve individual campsites. However, if you stop by the local Ranger's Office, you can find out where campsite vacancies exist. Group camp facilities can be reserved in a few Ranger Districts by contacting the Ranger's Office.

Many federal recreation areas charge a fee. The Golden Age (for persons over sixty-two) and Golden Access (for disabled persons) Passports allow free entrance to federally administered recreation areas and 50 percent discounts on fees for camping and swimming.

There are a few other general rules for camping in the

national forests. You must occupy your campsite the first night and not leave the site for more than twenty-four hours; your length of stay is limited to fourteen consecutive days; and fires are permitted only in stoves, grills, fireplaces, and fire rings.

JEKYLL ISLAND

Jekyll Island Campground
North Beachview Drive
Jekyll Island, GA 31520
912-635-3021

Jekyll Island is owned and operated by the state. The Jekyll Island Campground offers 200 sites on eighteen wooded acres not far from the beach. Operated by the Jekyll Island Authority, the campground features rest rooms, showers, pay phones, and laundry facilities. The camp store sells food, supplies, ice, propane gas, and minor trailer parts.

PRIVATE CAMPGROUNDS

Flat Creek Ranch Campground and Stables is a campground for equestrians, so there are facilities for campers as well as horses. Several annual equestrian events are held at the campground. Contact:

Flat Creek Stables
Hogansville, GA 30230
706-637-8920, 637-4862, or 637-8500

Hundreds of other chain and private campgrounds dot the state. For the most complete list, ask for the Department of Industry, Trade and Tourism's brochure "Camping in Georgia."

Department of Industry, Trade and Tourism
P.O. Box 1776
Atlanta, GA 30301-1776
404-656-3590

PRIMITIVE CAMPING

Cumberland Island National Seashore

National Park Service
P.O. Box 806
St. Marys, GA 31558
912-882-4335

For thousands of years small groups of people have lived on Cumberland Island, the largest and southernmost of Georgia's barrier islands. But because these groups have always been so small, the island has remained essentially unspoiled. At the turn of the century, the wealthy Carnegie family built several opulent homes scattered about the island. Today the estates are abandoned and mostly in ruins. In 1972, the Carnegie family donated both land and buildings to the National Park Foundation so that the island could become a National Seashore. That status ensures that Cumberland Island will always remain in its natural state.

The island is characterized by saltwater marshes, a thick maritime forest, forty-foot sand dunes, and a wide, flat, hard-packed beach. Visitors are likely to see wild turkeys, armadillos, white-tailed deer, feral pigs, alligators, and wild horses. The native bobcat was recently reintroduced but is seldom observed.

Camping on Cumberland Island is not for the faint-hearted, but it is free. Daily access to the island is stringently limited to 300 campers and day-trippers by advance reservation. Passage is only via a National Park Service ferry. With the exception of Park Service and a few private vehicles, no motor vehicles are permitted on the island. You have to walk everywhere you go. You must take—and be prepared to carry—every item you will need. No tents, sleeping bags, or other equipment is available for rent on the island, nor is there a store where you can buy food or supplies. Trash must be packed out.

Once on Cumberland Island, you can choose between one "developed" or four primitive backcountry sites, all of which are blessedly shady. The developed site, Sea Camp, has rest rooms, cold showers, safe drinking water, and a board-walk to the beach. Each campsite features a picnic table and a food cage (to foil clever raccoons). Campfires are permitted, but only dead and downed wood may be used.

The backcountry sites are located miles from the dock— Yankee Paradise, Hickory Hill, Brickhill Bluff, and Stafford Beach—and have NO facilities. Well water is available near each site, but it must be treated. Campfires are not permitted, so you must bring a camp stove (remember that you'll have to carry it to and from the site). You'll need to hang your food and trash in the trees and bury human waste.

Stafford Beach, located 3.5 miles north of Sea Camp, is suggested for novice backpackers and those who want easy access to the beach. Hickory Hill is 5.5 miles from Sea Camp,

Yankee Paradise is 7.4 miles, and Brickhill Bluff is 10.6 miles. Remember that you have to hike the same distance back to Sea Camp when you leave.

Sites are assigned at Sea Camp on arrival during a short orientation. Changing sites is not permitted. No more than twenty campers are allowed at any site. Campers lucky enough to get Sea Camp sites only have to carry their gear several hundred feet to the forest base camp in the live oaks adjacent to the beach. Carts are available to aid in transporting gear. All camping is limited to seven days.

Campers must have advance reservations, which can be obtained by calling 912-882-4335 weekdays. That's not as easy as it sounds. Reservations can only be made eleven months in advance. The competition for spaces is so intense you'll have to have an automatic redial feature on your phone to have any hope of getting through.

Reservations are required for space on the ferry whether you are a day-tripper or a camper. The ferry, the *Cumberland Queen*, operates two round-trips daily from St. Marys on the mainland from March 15 through September 30 and Thursday through Monday, October 1 through March 14. During certain peak periods a third round-trip is added. A fee is charged. The ferry does not carry cars, bicycles, or pets. Once at the island, the ferry stops at Sea Camp dock for campers and at Dungeness dock for day-trippers.

While on Cumberland Island you can fish (state fishing laws apply), hike, enjoy twenty miles of deserted beach, or observe the wildlife. Near the National Park Service dock is a small museum with artifacts tracing the history of the island. You'll want to hike to the various ruins. However, the remains of Dungeness and most of its outbuildings are unstable, so they are closed. Stafford, while still intact, is also closed, although you can look in the windows. Plum Orchard, which is in excellent condition and under restoration, is sometimes open for tours.

There are several rules you must keep in mind, and a few suggestions will make your stay more enjoyable. Stay off of the sand dunes and use only designated dune crossings. Walking on the dunes destroys vegetation, causes erosion, and disturbs nesting habitats for sea turtles and shorebirds. Living shells may not be taken.

During the summer it is best to visit the beach in the early morning or late in the day to avoid overexposure to the searing sun. For the sake of your feet, don't hike on the beach barefooted. Don't hike too far, and carry plenty of water—heat exhaustion is the most common first-aid problem. Use good-quality, lightweight hiking shoes or boots, and change socks frequently.

Feeding or capturing wildlife is prohibited. Diamondback rattlesnakes and three other types of poisonous snakes are found on the island, so be on the lookout. Ticks can be a problem. If horses congregate on the beach, it usually means that insects are bad inland, so you should probably head for the beach, too. There are no lifeguards, so exercise caution: never swim alone. Always watch for sharks. Emergency phones are located at Plum Orchard Mansion and the Sea Camp Visitor Center.

Don't forget to bring a flashlight, batteries, a first-aid kit, rope, sunscreen, sunglasses, insect repellent, comfortable walking shoes, rain gear, a camera, and film.

When you are returning to the mainland, the ferry leaves promptly on schedule, so be at the dock at least fifteen minutes early.

• If you are not an experienced primitive camper, backpacker, or hiker, we strongly suggest that you take a day trip to Cumberland Island to check it out. Even though we had read up on the island and its primitive camping sites, we had little conception of the distances involved or the lack of facilities until we had actually seen the sites for ourselves.

Okefenokee National Wildlife Refuge

U.S. Fish and Wildlife Service
Okefenokee National Wildlife Refuge
Route 2, Box 338
Folkston, GA 31537
912-496-3331

Camping at the mysterious Okefenokee Swamp is a real back-to-nature activity. First, you have to canoe from camping spot to camping spot. Just as at Cumberland Island, a camping experience in the swamp involves hauling everything you need with you. That chore should be considerably easier here than on Cumberland Island, but a canoe holds just so much.

Overnight camping is permitted at designated overnight stops only. Because there is little dry land, sites are generally twenty-foot by twenty-eight-foot covered wooden platforms on which you can set up a pop tent or jungle hammock. At least you won't have to sleep on the ground. Each site has docking facilities, but no water. Portable toilets with disposable bags are required, even though most overnight sites are outfitted with chemical toilets.

During your trip, you probably will not see any other humans besides those in your party. Each canoe trail—they range in length from fourteen miles (two days) to forty-three miles (five days)—is limited to one party per day. Each party is limited to ten canoes and/or twenty persons.

Camping parties are restricted to one night per site. For safety reasons, you must remain at the site between sunset and sunrise. Pets are not permitted, and swimming is prohibited because of potential danger from alligators. For the same reason, you should not trail fish you have caught on a stringer. A Coast Guard–approved life jacket, compass, and flashlight are required.

No nails can be used, nor can you cut trees or limbs when setting up your campsite. Open fires are not permitted, so gasoline, bottled gas, or similar types of stoves are required. Suggested supplies include a rope for pulling the canoe, drinking water, insect repellent, mosquito netting, rain gear, first-aid kit, extra batteries, litter bags, and a pop tent or jungle hammock and a sleeping bag.

Temperatures are hot and humid. Daily temperatures average above 90° F, with warm nights from June through September. Temperatures on winter days can range from 40° to 80° but are generally in the 50s and 60s, while nights can be near or below freezing. The rainy season is from June through September.

Mosquitoes can be a problem after dark from April through October. Deerflies are a biting menace during the summer but are not as bad deep in the swamp. There is no need to fear snakes as long as you take normal precautions.

Reservations can be made by telephone only, no earlier than two months to the day prior to your intended departure date. Call 912-496-3331 on weekdays.

In addition to the normal entrance fees to the swamp, a small, nonrefundable fee per person per night is charged for each member of the canoe party.

Canoes, camping equipment, and services are available for rent from the concessionaire at the Suwannee Canal Recreation Area at Folkston (912-496-7156) or the Stephen C.

Foster State Park at Fargo (912-637-5274). For information on canoe or equipment rentals, contact:

Carl Glenn, Jr., Concessionaire
Okefenokee National Wildlife Refuge
Suwannee Canal Recreation Concession, Inc.
Route 2, Box 336
Folkston, GA 31537
912-496-7156

If entering from the Fargo entrance, contact:

Stephen C. Foster State Park
(a primary entrance to the swamp)
Route 1, Box 131
Fargo, GA 31631
912-637-5274

CAMPING THROUGH A TOUR OPERATOR OR ORGANIZATIONS

Remember the old Greyhound Lines motto "Leave the driving to us"? You can experience the North Georgia mountains, Okefenokee Swamp, Cumberland Island and/or several of Georgia's other barrier islands while leaving all the details—and sometimes even most of the equipment—to someone else.

Medicine Bow
Route 8, Box 1780/Wahsega Road
Dahlonega, GA 30533
706-864-5928
Contact: Mark Warren

Medicine Bow, located in the North Georgia mountains, is an outdoor school for all ages that guides each student toward his or her unique relationship with the forest by connecting to the ancient skills and lore of Native Americans as they relate to food, medicine, tools, fire, art, shelter, and comfort.

Mark Warren is a lifelong student of nature and primitive lore. He served for ten years as a naturalist/environmentalist for the Georgia Conservancy and for seventeen years as Wilderness Director for High Meadows Camp. He is the author of *Magic from the Woods* and *The American Wilderness Awards Program.* In 1980 he designed and taught Georgia's first statewide environmental education workshops for public schools, for which he was named the National Wildlife Federation's Conservation Educator of the year.

Summer camp for boys and girls ten years old and up is a five-day session of primitive camping. In one of the three specialty camps—**Native American Camp, Archer Camp,** and **Explorer Camp**—children learn to think and act for themselves to meet their needs in the wild.

Weekend camps are held periodically throughout the year. **Parent Child Primordial Camp** is designed for quality family time in the adventures of spears, bows and arrows, games of action, stealth, and forest savvy. Participants supply their own camping gear and food.

Fall Weekend with the Earth involves an in-depth study of the autumn plants of southern Appalachia. Skills include how to identify plants and use them as food, medicine, and craft materials.

In **Tracking and Stalking Camp**, you'll learn animal gaits, prints and track patterns, how to read events and personalities on the Earth's surface, and how to get close to wild animals.

Survival Skills Camp teaches the secrets Native Americans use to stay alive comfortably. Participants learn such skills as carrying less gear as well as tips on shelter, fire, food, cooking, and attitude.

Winter Weekend with the Earth teaches how leafless plants can be identified and used. An in-depth study of fire includes instruction on how to create a fire by friction using materials found in the forest.

Other activities and skills taught at Medicine Bow include canoeing, archery, flute making, art with natural dyes, Indian sign language, hide tanning, and Native American ceremonies.

Wilderness Southeast
711 Sandtown Road
Savannah, GA 31410
912-897-5108

Wilderness Southeast is a nonprofit educational organization celebrating its twentieth anniversary. The enterprise, located near Savannah, sponsors several camping programs in Georgia, as well as throughout the United States and in foreign locations. While the leaders here stress physical activity and environmental awareness, their approach is not wilderness survival à la Outward Bound. You should be in reasonably good physical condition, but you don't need to be in training for the Olympics to participate. Attendees come from every age group, but the average age is about forty-five.

For programs that include canoeing, Wilderness Southeast provides canoes, paddles, life jackets, and seat cushions. Most programs include all meals and wine with dinner, tents with sewn-in floors, mosquito netting and rain flies, cleaning equipment, commissary gear, tarps, lanterns, first-aid and safety equipment, and with prior notice, even shuttle transportation from the nearest airport to the location. You provide, or can rent from them, a sleeping bag and Thermarest or foam sleeping pad. All you need to bring are a canteen, footwear, rain gear, clothing, and toiletries.

Wilderness Southeast's camping programs in Georgia are clustered around the coast and the least inhabited barrier islands, as explained below.

Sapelo Island. You'll be ferried from the mainland aboard the *Sapelo Queen* and transported to the "Big House" on the south end of the island. Built in 1807, the mansion now includes thirteen bedrooms, so you don't have to rough it. During the four-day excursion, you'll explore diverse island habitats and vast beaches, and visit a Guale Indian shell ring, the ruins of a French settlement called "Chocolate," and Hog Hammock, one of the few surviving island villages of slave descendants.

Cumberland Island. During this four-day trip, you'll visit visible remains from ancient Indian cultures, the Revolutionary War era, and the turn-of-the-century grandeur of the Carnegie period as well as a ridge of slowly migrating sand dunes encroaching upon an impressive live oak forest. You'll camp at Sea Camp, which offers a bathhouse and shower. (See above for a more complete description of Cumberland Island.)

Ossabaw Island. Purchased by the Torrey family in 1924 and later designated as Georgia's first Heritage Preserve, Ossabaw Island contains 25,000 acres rich in natural resources and cultural history. Access to the island is by twenty-minute boat ride. This program combines roughing it with Southern elegance and hospitality. The base camp—where you'll spend three days—is located in an ancient maritime forest on the south end of the island, where the beach is almost a half-mile wide at low tide. Here you'll learn skills such as how to pull a seine, throw a cast net, and run a crab line. If you're lucky, you'll get to watch sea turtles nesting and hatching. Then Mrs. Eleanor Torrey West welcomes you to her twelve-bedroom home, where you can experience the lifestyle and hospitality that characterized Georgia's turn-of-the-century island estates. The pace on the five-day trip is leisurely, and there are several hiking options.

Coastal Georgia Sea Kayak. Base camp is on Little Tybee Island, and there are day trips by kayak to Wassaw Island, a National Wildlife Refuge. Wilderness Southeast provides single and double kayaks and paddling gear. This is probably the most strenuous program the company offers. Some canoe or kayak experience is suggested, and participants need to be confident swimmers and in excellent health because they may be paddling against the wind or tide. Seafood lovers will think they've died and gone to heaven as they gather mussels, crabs, oysters, and fish for dinner.

Okefenokee Swamp. Wilderness Southeast offers three ways to explore the swamp.

Okefenokee Wilderness Canoe. The five-day program involves a day of hiking, during which you will identify swamp vegetation. During the succeeding days you will be canoeing; paddling distance varies from five to twelve miles per day. You'll camp on the periphery of the swamp as well as in the wilderness area on platforms. (See description above.)

Okefenokee Cabin/Canoe. This three-day program is an ideal itinerary for folks who wish to survey the swamp but who want to return to the comfort of a cabin at night. You'll paddle different trails every day (the maximum paddling distance is eight miles) as you examine life under the lily pads and investigate the significance of fire on the ecology of the swamp. In addition, you'll explore the once-thriving logging town on Billy's Island. The excursion involves a portage to the Suwannee River. Each night you'll stay in comfortable cabins with showers and full kitchen facilities at Stephen C. Foster State Park.

Photo Workshop. Limited to twelve, the group is accompanied by a Nikon representative. Instruction includes information about film types and equipment as well as tricks of the trade. The four-day excursion includes canoeing. Participants stay in cabins.

Coastal Experience. These summer camps are an adventure in learning for highly motivated students entering seventh, eighth, and ninth grades. Eight-day sessions begin at the Skidaway Marine Institute near Savannah, a Marine Extension Service of the University of Georgia. Facilities there include a 10,000-gallon aquarium, lecture rooms, two wet labs, and three dry labs. Students sleep in dormitories and eat in the cafeteria. Then they transfer to one of the barrier islands, where they camp in the forest near the beach. They'll sleep in two-person tents and cook on camp stoves. They need to be prepared to rough it because there are no bathroom facilities on the island.

Sea Turtle Watch. The act of turtles laying their eggs on the beach is a prehistoric ritual reenacted on southeastern beaches every night in June and July. Participants in this five-day program will help teams of sea turtle researchers patrol the beaches in search of the endangered reptiles so they can collect data on nesting patterns as well as protect the nests. You need to be able to walk the 2.5 miles of beach several times each night. You'll sleep in a rustic, one-room dormitory with one bathroom and an outdoor shower.

Other places that offer primitive camping include McIntosh Reserve (weekends only), Hidden Creek Campground,

Cohutta Wilderness Area, and the Flint River Outdoor Center. (See Chapter 11, "Special Places," for additional information.)

Overnight trail rides (See Chapter 5)
White water/camping (See Chapter 9)
Fishing camp (See Chapter 3)

3 FISHING

At the risk of offending aficionados, we have to admit that fishing (and we've tried deep-sea, surf, and fresh-water fishing) is about as exciting as watching grass grow. However, we know that's a very unpopular opinion, so for those of you who are ardent fans of the sport, here's what we've found out.

Fishing, among all the other outdoor pursuits, is the one in which just about anyone can participate regardless of age, physical condition, athletic ability, or strength.

Georgia offers a wide range of fishing experiences, from deep-sea and surf casting along the coast to angling in the coastal marshes and the state's many rivers and lakes. Trout fishing in the tumbling waters of the North Georgia mountains is an extremely popular activity.

Your best source of fishing information is the Georgia Department of Natural Resources (DNR), Game and Fish Division. The people there publish the yearly fishing regulations and even put out free "Annual Fishing Predictions" booklets by area of the state. About the only thing they don't do is bait your hook for you.

The Fisheries people tell us that more than 1.5 million people fish in Georgia's waters annually—that's 78,000 anglers a day. The average angler fishes twenty-two days a year and spends about 5.5 hours each trip.

If you want to contact the Game and Fish Division, you can do so at several locations, including Atlanta, 404-656-3524; Albany, 912-430-4256; Calhoun, 706-629-1259; Fort Valley, 912-825-7841; Gainesville, 404-535-5498; Savannah, 912-727-2112; Social Circle, 404-656-4817; and Waycross, 912-285-6094.

FISHING ALONG THE COAST

According to the DNR, over three million fish are caught annually in Georgia's six coastal counties—Bryan, Camden, Chatham, Glynn, Liberty, and McIntosh. These counties stretch along the mainland from Savannah to St. Marys and include several barrier islands—Tybee, Wilmington, Blackbeard, St. Simons, Little St. Simons, Sea, Sapelo, St. Catherines, Cumberland, and Jekyll. No fishing license is required for fishing in saltwater.

Over 400,000 acres of rich salt marsh produce many types of recreational fish. Inshore fishermen angle for spotted sea trout, red drum, croaker, whiting, and flounder. Sea trout are available year-round, but, in general, inshore fishing is best from mid-May through December with variations depending on the type of fish: whiting from mid-April through May, red drum from September through December, sheepshead during warm months, and black drum during fall.

41

The following hints are offered for inshore fishing: sheepshead and black drum gather around bridge and pier pilings; black drum are found at bridges crossing deep river channels during late spring and early summer.

Crabbing is a popular activity for the whole family. The only equipment you need is a crab trap and a chicken back for bait, or you can use a string, bait, and a long-handled net. If you're using a trap, all you have to do is lower it to the bottom. The trap opens to make the bait accessible. After a few minutes, all you have to do is pull it up full of trapped crabs. If you're using a baited string and a net, when you feel the crab start moving off with the bait, you slowly bring in your line until the crab is visible, then scoop it up with your net.

Offshore fishermen go for king mackerel, snapper, grouper, cobia, shark, and black sea bass. In February and March, fishing with fiddler crabs can attract sheepshead and sea bass. Bluefish migrate north in April, while cobia collect around buoys and artificial reefs in May. Black sea bass bite best in summer in deep water (100 feet or deeper) or in winter in close offshore waters; triggerfish bite best in summer bottom fishing.

A very special offshore fishing site is Gray's Reef National Marine Sanctuary. Located seventeen miles east of Sapelo Island, it is the only nearby reef with a natural live bottom area.

The DNR has constructed several offshore artificial reefs and several inshore artificial reefs. Located twelve miles out, the offshore reefs are in forty-five feet of water. Half are north and half are south of the St. Simons Channel. Identified by yellow, state-maintained buoys, the offshore reefs are popular because they are closest to shore for deep-sea fishing, providing the opportunity for half-day rather full-day charters.

Otherwise, you'll have to travel twenty-five miles out to sea, requiring a full day.

Typical fish caught at the reefs include Spanish mackerel, king mackerel, barracuda, amberjack, bonita, and cobia. Fishermen tell us that cobia, which average thirty to thirty-five pounds, are the most fun to catch because of the fight they put up. For cobia, thirty-three inches is the minimum legal length. Cobia are caught only in late spring/early summer and late fall/early winter.

Fishing guide Johnbird Daniel told us that the best way to find cobia is to look near structures or buoys or if you see rays.

Both inshore and offshore waters can yield sharks. Several small varieties (two to four feet long) congregate in sounds and ship channels during the summer. Larger varieties are found in offshore waters.

SURF FISHING OFF THE BARRIER ISLANDS

Georgia's numerous barrier islands offer miles and miles of beach from which to fish. Some restrictions apply: surf fishing at the north end of Sea Island in the Hampton River is limited to residents.

The only access to Cumberland Island is via reservation on the National Park Service ferry; only 300 campers and day-trippers are permitted on the island daily. If you're one of the lucky ones, you could have twenty miles of deserted hard-packed beach for your private fishing grounds. Cast into the surf or the sound for red bass, sea trout, bluefish, croaker, and drum. A 1.5-mile jetty juts out into the ocean, providing excellent fishing for reds, mullet, trout, and even shrimp. Light tackle only is permitted.

Fishing piers are available for nonboaters at Lazaretto Creek (Tybee Island Causeway) and Tybee Island, Back River and McKay River (both on St. Simons Causeway), Blythe Island Regional Park, Jekyll Island, and St. Simons Island. Boat ramp/floating docks are available at Port Wentworth, Tivoli River, Riceboro River Bridge, Blue-N-Hall, Harris Neck, and Crooked River State Park.

Most piers offer rod rentals, charts, diesel fuel, gas, oil, ice, and bait as well as boat launching and dockage.

Fishing spots with access for disabled people are addressed in the section on sporting opportunities for the disabled in Chapter 10, "Something for Everyone."

Fishing is permitted at these coastal National Wildlife Refuges: Blackbeard Island, Harris Neck, Savannah, and Okefenokee.

For more information and an excellent brochure called "Coastal Georgia Fishing," contact one of the following addresses:

Coastal Georgia Regional Development Center
P.O. Box 1917
Brunswick, GA 31521
912-264-7363

Georgia Department of Natural Resources
Coastal Resources Division
1200 Glynn Avenue
Brunswick, GA 31523-9990
912-264-7218

For information on fish and fishing methods, seasons, and exact locations, maps are available (for a small fee) by county from:

University of Georgia Marine Extension Service
P.O. Box Z
Brunswick, GA 31523

COASTAL OFFSHORE OUTFITTERS/CHARTERS

Tybee Island Charters
P.O. Box 1762
Tybee Island, GA 31328
912-786-4801
Contact: Cecil and Elizabeth Johnson

Located on the island near Savannah, the charter company offers trips that range from four to fifteen hours. The four-, six-, and eight-hour trips go about fifteen miles offshore, while the eleven- and fifteen-hour trips range from forty-five to sixty miles offshore. The company will also guide anglers on inshore fishing trips. The thirty-foot boat accommodates up to six people. Bait, tackle, and ice are provided.

Coastal Boating Academy
204 Golden Isles Marina
St. Simons, GA 31522
912-638-7717

This outfit offers inshore and offshore fishing.

Larry Kennedy Charters
Hampton River Club Marina
St. Simons, GA 31522
912-638-3214

Larry Kennedy is an Orvis-endorsed guide. He has been fishing the local coastal waters for forty years and offers instruction in fly, spin, and conventional angling. His specialty is release fishing for tarpon, shark, reds, and trout.

Vicki Ann Charters
Golden Isles Marina
St. Simons, GA 31522
912-638-0001

Vicki Ann's thirty-foot cruiser can handle up to six persons for full-day fishing charters that run twenty-five to forty miles offshore.

Jekyll Island Wharf
#1 Pier Road
Jekyll Island, GA 31520
912-635-2891

The wharf offers a 10.5-hour deep-sea fishing trip to a forty-mile reef noted for grouper, red snapper, black sea bass, amberjack, kingfish, dolphin, and barracuda. All you have to bring is your own lunch. Beer and soft drinks are sold on board. In addition, the wharf offers offshore trolling twenty-five to forty miles off the coast for king mackerel, barracuda, bonita, amberjack, and dolphin. Shark fishing is available. Bring a box lunch and beverages. Five-, eight-, ten-, and twelve-hour trips are offered.

COASTAL INSHORE OUTFITTERS/CHARTERS

Jekyll Island Wharf
#1 Pier Road

Jekyll Island, GA 31520
912-635-2891

Jekyll Island Wharf (opposite) offers full- and half-day guided trips on the Intracoastal Waterway to fish for trout, bass, flounder, and whiting.

Inland Charter Boat Service
North First Street
P.O. Box 11
Sea Island, GA 31561
912-638-3611, Ext. 5202
Contact: Frank and Janet Mead

The charter service offers half-day fishing trips to the Hampton, Village, and Black Banks rivers, located between St. Simons, Little St. Simons, and Sea Islands. The service has a roster of well-known charter guides. Fishing is for speckled sea trout, redfish or channel bass, flounder, whiting, sheepshead, croaker, drum, and spot all year. Speckled trout are most plentiful in late April and in October and November. The service also offers half-day excursions for tarpon and shark, generally between June and September.

At the dock on the grounds of Sea Island's Cloister Resort, you can rent rods and bait. In addition, the location is ideal for catching small spot, croaker and catfish. Inland also rents crab traps and bait. For fishing trips, reservations are required.

FISHING IN RIVERS AND STREAMS

According to the DNR, Fisheries Section, Georgia has more than 12,000 miles of warm-water streams (as opposed to the

47

cold-water streams in the northern part of the state) that support large populations of black bass, bream, crappie, and several catfish species. Each mile of warm-water stream supports 1,200 hours of fishing annually. Large rivers such as the Altamaha support 1,700 hours, but even more popular are the North Georgia trout streams that receive 10,000 hours. The Fisheries Management Section stocks the mountain trout streams that we'll talk about later.

There is no closed season for fishing in streams, reservoirs, lakes, and ponds in Georgia, with the following exceptions:

• Trout streams designated as seasonal (see trout section).
• Certain sections of the Flint River, the Chattahoochee River, and Spring Creek are closed to striped bass and spear fishing part of the year.
• A section of the Savannah River is closed to striped bass and hybrid striped bass/white bass fishing.

Most of the bass fishing done in South Georgia occurs on the Altamaha River, the largest watershed east of the Mississippi. Based on data from bass fishing tournaments, more participants caught their limit of fish on the Altamaha than on any other body of water in Georgia. Bluegill and flathead catfish (Appaloosas) are prevalent throughout the Altamaha.

The Fisheries Section calls the following areas outstanding: Jaycee's Landing, the area of Strickland Bight and the "cut thru" of Marrowbone, and the entire river section in and around Upper Eason's Bluff Landing.

Other outstanding fishing rivers in the southeastern region of the state include the Ocmulgee for catfish; Oconee for largemouth bass; Ogeechee for redbreast sunfish, bluegill, redear sunfish (shellcracker), and black crappie; Satilla for redbreast sunfish, bluegill, and largemouth bass; Savannah for redbreast sunfish, channel catfish, black crappie, and yellow perch; St. Marys for redbreast sunfish and bass, and the Suwannee for chain pickerel, warmouth, and flier (shiner). Other rivers and streams noted for good fishing include Seventeen-Mile River, Flint River, Ochlocknee River, Kinchafoonee Creek, and Toccoa River.

FISHING IN INLAND LAKES AND RESERVOIRS

Georgia's 500,000 acres of impounded waters and reservoirs offer some of the best fishing in the Southeast. These bodies of water are known for black bass, bream, crappie, and catfish as well as striped bass and striped bass/white bass hybrids. The vast majority of Georgia's fishermen (82 percent) do their angling in reservoirs and ponds.

The Game and Fish Division operates ten **Public Fishing Areas** that are managed intensively. Fish species available include largemouth bass, bream (bluegill and redear sunfish), channel catfish, and crappie. Some of these are closed part of the year. A Wildlife Management Area stamp is required in addition to a fishing license.

The Public Fishing Areas are: Arrowhead, 706-295-6023; Baldwin Forest, 912-453-4200; Big Lazer Creek, 912-995-4486; Big Hammock, 912-423-2988; Dodge County, 912-374-0651; Evans County, 912-739-1139; McDuffie, 706-595-1684; Paradise, 912-533-4792; Rum Creek, 912-825-7841; and Treutlen, 912-685-6424.

The state is currently developing 5,000 acres called Marben/Clybel Farms. This recently acquired area north of Monticello in Central Georgia contains twenty-eight manmade ponds totaling 300 acres of water. Many of these lakes are noted for outstanding fishing. For example, largemouth bass in excess of ten pounds have been landed as well as large bluegill and shellcracker. Right now the lakes are fishable only by boat, but future plans include extensive improvements.

The state also operates nine fish hatcheries: Bowens Mill, 912-423-7211; Buford (trout), 706-889-1150; Burton (trout), 706-947-3122; Cordele, 912-276-2362; Richmond Hill, 912-756-3691; Steve Cocke, 912-995-4486; Summerville, 706-857-3394; and Walton, 404-656-4817.

FISHING AT STATE PARKS AND HISTORIC SITES

Georgia State Parks and Historic Sites
1352 Floyd Tower East
205 Butler Street, S.E.
Atlanta, GA 30334
404-656-3520

Eleven of Georgia's state parks are located on major lakes and reservoirs with outstanding fishing, including Lakes Alla-toona, Burton, Clarks Hill, George, Hartwell, Russell, and Seminole. These parks offer boat ramps and docks. Several have marinas supplying fuel, groceries, and boating supplies. They are open all year except for Lake Seminole, where all fishing (including spear fishing) for any species in marked areas around five fish refuges is closed part of the year. Twenty-six other parks are located on smaller lakes with excellent fishing. Most have boat ramps and docks; many offer boat and canoe rentals.

Private boats are permitted in some park waters, but some of the smaller lakes have restrictions on private boats and/or horsepower limitations.

There are no fees for fishing in park lakes, rivers, or

streams. However, a valid Georgia fishing license is required for fishermen over sixteen. Trout stamps are required when fishing in streams.

Georgia Department of Industry, Trade and Tourism
P.O. Box 1776
Atlanta, GA 30301-1776
404-656-3590

The department publishes an excellent brochure called "Fishing in Georgia" that lists all the state's major lakes, including location, acreage, fish types found there, a phone contact, and whether that lake offers boating, camping, picnic areas, public beaches, and/or marinas.

FISHING IN THE AUGUSTA CANAL

Augusta Canal Authority
801 Broad Street, Room 507
Augusta, GA 30901
706-722-1071

The nine-mile Augusta Canal was built in 1846 to provide transportation for the many mills along the Savannah River. From the very first, however, the canal provided recreational activities as well.

The fish ladder allows striped bass, hybrid bass, white bass, and American shad to continue upriver to their spawning grounds—providing good fishing year-round. Other common fish are black bass, yellow perch, catfish, shellcracker, bluegill, redbreasted bream, and longnose and spotted gar.

FISHING IN THE OKEFENOKEE SWAMP

Sport fishing is permitted during posted hours in accordance with Georgia State Law and refuge regulations. Live minnows are not permitted as bait. Another very practical tip we picked up while visiting the Swamp was not to keep your catch on a stringer. Alligators consider a stringer full of fish an invitation to dinner and have been known to consume an entire catch, stringer and all. In addition, it is no fun having an alligator that close to your boat, so use a bait box. Bass fishing is best in early spring and late fall depending on water level, moon phase, and weather. For more information, contact:

Okefenokee National Wildlife Refuge
U.S. Fish and Wildlife Service
Route 2, Box 338
Folkston, GA 31537
912-496-3331

Suwannee Canal Recreation Concessions, Inc.
Route 2, Box 336
Folkston, GA 31537
912-496-7156

Stephen C. Foster State Park
Route 1, Box 131
Fargo, GA 31631
912-637-5274

PRIVATE LAKE GUIDES/OUTFITTERS

Wingate's Bass Island Campground/
Jack Wingate's Lunker Lodge
Route 1, Box 3311
Bainbridge, GA 31717
912-246-0658

This complex, under one ownership, offers a wide range of fishing experiences. The campground, at Hutchinson Ferry Landing on Lake Seminole, provides year-round camping with water and light hookups, a central dumping station, a shower and rest room building, washers and dryers, a playground, and a fishing pier. Every campsite has a view of the lake. In fact, you can beach your boat in front of your campsite.

Lunker Lodge has sixteen motel rooms, while the Stag Hangout houses groups of up to eighteen men. The Lunker Lodge store carries fishing tackle, gasoline, ice, and groceries. Folks come from miles around to eat catfish and barbecue at the restaurant.

During the summer a week-long camp for boys, ages nine to fifteen, provides instruction in fishing, water sports, marksmanship, woodcraft, and the history of the area.

LaPrade's
Route 1, State 197N
Clarkesville, GA 30523
706-947-3312

Mayo's Lock and Dam
181 Lock and Dam Road
Rome, GA 30161
706-234-5001

Mayo's offers fishing, boating, picnicking, and RV campsites.

IN SEARCH OF TROUT

Above all of the others, the most sought-after species in the state is trout—rainbow, brown, and brook or speckled. Georgia offers 4,000 miles of streams, rivers, and brooks officially designated as trout water. These streams are frequented by 100,000 anglers yearly. For the beginner, the Fisheries Section of the DNR puts out a publication called "Introduction to Georgia Trout Streams."

You have to work extra hard for the prized native brook trout because they are found primarily in feeder streams and headwaters accessible only by hiking. However, once you're on the scene, the "brookie" is easy to catch with a wide variety of baits, including small spinning lures and artificial flies.

Popular because of their spectacular jumps, long runs, and fighting style, rainbows are stocked by fish hatcheries to supplement the native population.

The most widespread trout is the brown trout, which can also be found in the warmer waters south of the mountains. The brown is attracted to flies, spinning lures, and live bait. Because this trout is wary and easily spooked, he's not caught as often, so many grow to be trophy size.

Most of the state's trout streams are located within the Chattahoochee National Forest. The U.S. Forest Service offers a map of the forest designating trout waters for a small fee. Call 404-536-0541. The Georgia Department of Natural Resources puts out a free brochure called "Guide to Georgia Trout Regulations." Call 404-656-3524 for a copy.

The official trout season runs from the last Saturday in March to October 31. However, a few streams are open for trout fishing year-round. With the exception of Rock Creek

54

Lake and Dockery Lake, the Georgia Trout Season does not apply to any lake or reservoir.

TROUT FISHING ON STOCKED STREAMS

The following streams are stocked and easily accessible.

Habersham County: **Panther Creek** is located along US 441 north of Clarkesville. Trout are stocked every other week during the season. The stream is open year-round below the mouth of Little Panther Creek. There is an excellent hiking trail along most of the stream.

Lumpkin County: **Dicks Creek** is located on Forest Service Road 34, off US 19 and US 129 northwest of Cleveland. It is stocked weekly during the season. Some of the lower part of the stream is on private land. Camping is available nearby. **Nimblewill Creek** is located on Forest Service Road 28, off State 52 west of Dahlonega. It is stocked every other week during the season. Some sections are on private land.

Rabun County: The **Tallulah River** is off US 76 and Forest Service Road 70 west of Clayton. It is heavily stocked every week. Two Forest Service campgrounds and one private one are located nearby.

Wildcat Creek is located on Forest Service Road 26, off State 197 north of Clarkesville in the Lake Burton Wildlife Management Area. It is stocked every week. Forest Service, state, and private camping are available nearby.

Stephens County: **Middle Fork/Broad River** is located on Forest Service Road 61, off US 123 east of Cornelia in the Lake Russell Wildlife Management Area. It is stocked every week. A Forest Service campground is located at Lake Russell.

Union County: **Coopers Creek**, on Forest Service Road 236, off State 60 between Blue Ridge and Dahlonega, is heavily stocked each week. In addition, you'll find a good population of wild rainbow and brook trout in the upper section of the main stream and the tributaries. The U.S. Forest Service operates two campgrounds nearby.

White County: The **Chattahoochee River** on Forest Service Road 52, off State 75 north of Helen, is heavily stocked weekly at several access points in the Chattahoochee Wildlife Management Area. You'll also find wild rainbows and browns. Some of the small tributaries offer native brook trout. Camping options include primitive camping, commercial campgrounds, and Unicoi State Park.

Smith Creek, on State 356, off State 75 north of Helen, is stocked weekly. The stream flows through Unicoi State Park. In fact, Unicoi Lake and Anna Ruby Falls, the spectacular double falls, are on the stream.

Georgia has many other stocked streams.

TROUT FISHING ON WILDERNESS STREAMS

These streams are in rugged terrain, not easily accessible by road, and not easy to fish. Plan your trip carefully, use a map and compass, and check with outfitters, the Forest Service, or local Chambers of Commerce before venturing out. And, of course, don't travel alone.

Waters Creek Trophy Trout Stream

Georgia Department of Natural Resources
Game and Fish Division
2123 US 278, S.E.

Social Circle, GA 30279
or call the Fisheries Office at Gainesville, 706-535-5498, or at
Burton, 706-947-3112.

The foremost wilderness stream is **Waters Creek Trophy
Trout Stream** in Lumpkin County. This "fish-for-fun" stream
is located on Forest Service Road 34, off US 129 north of
Cleveland in the Chestatee Wildlife Management Area in the
picturesque mountains of northern Lumpkin County. Fish are
rarely stocked here, but the forest service maintains a high-
density trout population in a 2.5-mile section of this stream by
feeding the fish and protecting them with very restrictive
regulations. Wild rainbow trout are the most abundant, but
you'll also find brown and brook trout.

Brown and rainbow trout must measure at least twenty-
two inches; brook trout, eighteen inches. The stream is intended for experienced anglers who are willing to release
their catch unharmed. Daily possession limit is one fish per
day; the seasonal limit is three trout per person. Only artificial
lures with a single barbless hook are allowed.

Waters Creek is open only on weekends and Wednesdays
from thirty minutes before sunrise until 6:30 P.M. EST (7:30
P.M. EDT). Anglers must check in and out at a check station.
A Wildlife Management Area stamp is required in addition
to the regular fishing license and trout stamp, except for
Honorary License holders. There are no developed facilities,
and parking is limited to pullouts along gravel roads. Other
trout fishing is available nearby at Dicks Creek.

Other Wilderness Streams

Also in Lumpkin County, **Jones Creek** is located on Forest
Service Road 77, off State 52 west of Dahlonega in the Blue

Ridge Wildlife Management Area. This is one of the state's best wild brown trout streams and is not stocked. Only artificial lures are allowed. The stream is not recommended for novice fishermen.

An excellent challenge is fishing on the **Chattooga River** in Rabun County, which straddles the Georgia/North Carolina border. Designated as a Wild and Scenic River, it first became well known because of the movie *Deliverance*. In addition to good fishing, the river offers many rafting, canoeing, and kayaking adventures. A reciprocal agreement between the two states allows anglers licensed in either state to fish from the banks of either side of the river.

The section between Burrell's Ford Bridge and State 28 on Forest Service Road 646 east of Clayton is stocked with sub-adult rainbow and brown trout. The stream is rugged and remote, but most of it is accessible by hiking trails.

The West Fork section on State 28 and Forest Service Road 86 is stocked every other week. The upper section is relatively inaccessible but offers good rainbow fishing for those intrepid enough to hike into the area.

SMALL LAKES WITH TROUT FISHING

There are many small impoundments that can be fished from the bank or from a canoe or float tube. **Nancytown Lake** in Habersham County is located on Forest Service Road 61, off US 123 east of Cornelia. It is stocked during the first part of trout season. Fishing is permitted year-round. You can also expect to find a good population of bass and bream.

Dockery Lake on State 60 north of Dahlonega in Lumpkin County is stocked every other week during trout season, which is the only time fishing is permitted.

Lake Winfield Scott on State 180 south of Blairsville in Union County is stocked every other week during the season. The lake is also good for bass and bream.

TROUT FISHING REGULATIONS

"Guide to Georgia Trout Regulations"
Georgia Department of Natural Resources
Game and Fish Division
Suite 1358, Floyd Towers East
205 Butler Street, S.E.
Atlanta, GA 30334
404-656-3524

Trout regulations may vary from area to area, but, in general, the following rules apply:

- Trotlines, set hooks, jugs, nets, bows and arrows, and all other gear except poles and lines are prohibited.
- Trout fishermen are restricted to the use of one pole and line, which must be hand-held.
- Live bait is prohibited.
- Some streams are designated as "artificial only" lures.
- Abide by minimum size requirements.
- It is illegal to move trout from one body of water to another.
- It is prohibited to continue fishing after the creel limit of eight per day has been reached.
- Fishing hours on streams with a season are thirty minutes before sunrise to thirty minutes after sunset. Night fishing is permitted on year-round streams.
- Certain streams or portions of streams have special

management programs and restrictions. They are the Chatta-hoochee River, Coleman River, Hoods Creek, Jones Creek, Moccasin Creek, Mountaintown Creek, Noontootla Creek, Stanley Creek, Walnut Fork Creek, and Waters Creek.

TROUT FISHING GUIDES AND OUTFITTERS

North Georgia Trout Adventures
41 River Street
Ellijay, GA 30540
706-635-3474

Trout Adventures offers guided fishing experiences designed for one or two people. Transportation is supplied from the base location to and from the native trout stream. You'll get a lesson, a full day of fishing, lunch, and the use of all fishing equipment. Trips are available during trout season, March 31 through September 30.

Host Mark Pinson, a native of the North Georgia moun-tains, has been doing research on native trout for fifteen years. His favorite fishing spots are Rock Creek, Noontootla Creek and its tributaries, Conasauga River and its tributaries, and Turniptown Creek.

Metro Guide Service
404-781-4847 (if there's no answer, leave a message)

Sponsored by the Chattahoochee Outdoor Center in coopera-tion with the National Park Service, this service provides guided fishing trips on the Chattahoochee River in north metro Atlanta. Some sections of the river are open to trout fishing all year, although the trout season is from March 31 to

October 31. The trip is for a minimum of four hours. Rates are for one or two people, and all tackle, bait, and lures are included. Fish are cleaned and bagged for free; pictures are taken for a nominal fee. A valid Georgia fishing license and a trout stamp are required. A 10 percent discount is offered to military and law enforcement personnel. Make reservations at least two weeks in advance.

Phil Davis, owner of the service, is the only licensed, insured, full-time guide in the area. He has twenty-eight years' experience.

Andy's Trout Farms
Box 129
Dillard, GA 30537
706-746-2550

If you don't want to work too hard getting to a good trout stream or you're afraid of going home empty handed, you might prefer Andy's. Several heavily stocked ponds and a lake ensure that every fisherman will be successful at catching some rainbows. Fish are sold by the pound. Bring your own equipment or rent it from them. No license is required. If you have any energy left over, Andy's features square dancing every night. Once you're finally tired, you can bunk down in one of his one- or two-bedroom cabins.

FLY FISHING INSTRUCTION

Callaway Gardens Resort
P.O. Box 2000
Pine Mountain, GA 31822
800-282-8181

"Anything that will eat another fish, you can catch with a fly rod," says Callaway Gardens Resort's instructor Truell Myers. He makes it sound so easy. Actually he got us to make passable casts, and that was a chore.

The resort offers several individual and group instructional options as well as guided fly-fishing excursions. Instruction includes fly-fishing techniques using wet and dry flies for a variety of freshwater species. Knots and equipment selection are also covered. After instruction on dry land and at the water's edge, anglers graduate to boats and/or float tubes.

Saturday clinics for up to ten people last six hours; lunch and beverages are provided. Reservations are required. The two-day schools provide ten hours of instruction. Once you've perfected your technique, you can take a half- or full-day guided excursion for morning or evening. Reservations are required.

The biggest lake at Callaway Gardens is Mountain Creek Lake, with 175 acres stocked with various varieties of game fish. This lake is open to individual anglers. The resort has twelve other private lakes for which you must have a guide to fish. Bass and brim are the most commonly caught fish.

The Boathouse can supply fully equipped tackle bags, rods and reels, and fishing boats with trolling motors for individual fishermen.

OTHER HELPFUL INFORMATION

"Fishing Hot Spots"
Jim Gebhard
726 Chamblin Road
Grovetown, GA 30813
800-338-5957

"Fishing Hot Spots" is a terrific set of maps of lakes and rivers featuring tips from local experts; boat landing locations; fishery survey results; migration patterns; stocking reports; forage base; location; access; related services such as boat rentals, bait shops, resorts, public parks, campgrounds, and guide services; special features of the lake, as well as lake characteristics including size and depth, water source, shoreline, bottom, water, and vegetation. The maps are waterproof and tearproof; they even float. Jim also produces the "Discoveries in Fishing" catalog.

Another source of information is the **"C. E. Smith Lakes & Rivers Guide"** (13375 Providence Road, Alpharetta, GA 30201, 404-475-2315).

Broadway Bait & Tackle & Rod & Reel Repair
Chris Jenkins
P.O. Box 1331
32 Eighth Street, Suite 200
Augusta, GA 30903-1331
800-726-0243 or 706-823-6600

Conveniently located next to the Augusta Canal, Broadway is the largest inshore tackle shop in the Southeast. The shop also rents canoes.

SPECIAL EVENTS

Hundreds of fishing meets attract anglers throughout the year. Lake Seminole's Lunker Lodge is the site of several national tournaments. In addition, the Game and Fish Division, DNR, sponsors special competitions such as Kids Fishing Events and Handicapped Persons Fishing Events.

4
HIKING

We'd been hiking with our dog for quite some time, enjoying the crisp air, blue sky, and the crunch of brittle leaves beneath our feet. We were almost at the foot of Horse Trough Falls when the first shot rang out. A hunter on the ridge above us had no idea we were below him. Shooting continued. We felt surrounded. Despite the fear and the rush of adrenaline, we started making mental notes of our baker's dozen hiking rules for trekking in the North Georgia mountains.

Rule 1: Don't go hiking during hunting season. Check ahead to see when various seasons are scheduled. If you go anyway, at least wear bright colors (and put a bright kerchief on your dog), keep to the trails, and stay out of thickly wooded areas. Fortunately, our hunter moved off in the opposite direction, and we beat a hasty retreat.

HIKING TO GEORGIA'S WATERFALLS

We like to have a destination when we hike, and Georgia's waterfalls make perfect targets. Most of them are located in national forest scenic or recreation areas or in state parks. Some demand some serious hiking and aren't for the faint-hearted, while others require little effort.

Rule 2: Be leery of directions to waterfalls. We rarely find a waterfall exactly where the map or directions say it is. In our experience, the people who write the directions either feel that part of the enjoyment of seeing a waterfall is making an adventure of finding it, or they are over seven feet tall, take forty-inch steps, drive a four-wheel drive vehicle with oversized tires (which throws the car's odometer off), and just don't see the world through the same eyes we mortals do. We call this the Paul Bunyan Syndrome.

We're middle-aged and in middling physical condition. We like to hike, but we get no enjoyment from struggling down sheer cliff faces, nor do we leap small mountains in a single bound. This is not to say that hiking is only for super jocks. North Georgia has something for everyone, from novice to expert backpacker. In addition, you can camp, fish, picnic, birdwatch, take pictures, or go horseback riding or mountain biking.

While you are there, don't miss these waterfalls:

Spectacular **Amicalola Falls**, with a dramatic drop of 729 feet, is the highest waterfall in Georgia. It is located in the state park of the same name on Springer Mountain at the southern end of the Appalachian Trail, 20 miles west of Dahlonega on State 52.

If you're more interested in the view than in the exercise, you can drive by paved road to the base of the falls, where

65

you can admire it while relaxing by a reflecting pool. Another paved road will take you to an overlook at the top for a completely different aspect of the falls, as well as a panorama of mountains and forests.

For the more exercise-oriented, a paved path meanders up the side of the falls. It is steep and contains numerous sets of rock stairs that can be treacherous when they're wet. Several overlooks along the way provide views of various cascades and provide much-sought-after resting places.

The West Ridge Loop Trail is an easy stroll through the woods. Because it is popular and easily accessible, Amicalola Falls is often crowded.

The top of the path to **Dukes Creek Falls,** in the Chattooga Ranger District, is easily accessible by road via the Richard Russell Scenic Highway north of Helen. Once long, rough, and tortuous, the trail has been graded and graveled. With the addition of numerous switchbacks, stairs, and benches, it is now moderately difficult. You'll know you've exerted yourself, though. The .8-mile descent seems longer than it is, and the way back up seems even longer.

If you're thinking about taking a picnic with you, use a backpack or fannypack. Otherwise, you'll soon be tempted to abandon anything you're carrying by hand. Once at the bottom, you'll have an awe-inspiring sight of the 300-foot drop and rugged boulders that seem to have been tossed there by some giant hand. The craggy scenery is a photographer's dream.

We'll never forget the time we went to Dukes Creek Falls with some of our grown children. One daughter (a female cross between Saint Francis of Assisi and James Herriot) had brought along an orphaned baby goat (she was bottle-feeding it and didn't want to leave it at home alone). She ended up walking it on a leash. Being a goat, it was more sure-footed than we were, but being so young, it got tired. On the way back up, we had to take turns carrying it. You can't imagine the looks and reactions we got from other hikers. "What kind of a dog is that?" "Will you take our picture with the . . . whatever it is?"

Anna Ruby Falls, in the Chattooga Ranger District, consists of two falls—one plummeting 153 feet, the other cascading down 50 feet. A steep, but paved, half-mile trail with several rest stops takes you to the falls, where an observation deck unveils a splendid view.

Difficult to find, but worth the effort, are **Helton Creek Falls** and **Horse Trough Falls**. Helton Creek Falls consists of three separate falls and an enchanting pool at the middle one. It is located in the Brasstown Ranger District north of Dahlonega on US 19 between DeSoto Falls and Vogel State Park.

No sign announces the existence of Helton Creek Falls. The dirt road is identified by a regular green-and-white street sign—Helton Creek Falls Road. Drive through a wooded residential neighborhood of rustic houses; then continue down the mountain about a mile. You won't find parking areas, signs, or obvious path entrances to indicate the way to the falls. Park at wide spots along the road and look for trail entrances. You can just hear the falls from the road. Once you've found one of the falls, you can work your way up or downstream to the others.

Horse Trough Falls, in the Chattooga Ranger District, is for the serious waterfall enthusiast. You need to be determined and intrepid. It's not that the path itself is difficult; it's getting to the path that's such a challenge. North of Helen on State 75, you turn onto a one-lane dirt forest service road identified by a minute sign—#44, Wilkes Creek Road.

A four-wheel-drive vehicle would be ideal for this road is

extremely rough. Our low-slung sedan was not pleased with being tortured. We took several wrong turns because there are no signs. Take the right fork when the road makes a sharp left curve at the bottom of the canyon.

You'll soon get to a shallow stream that doesn't have the one-lane wooden bridge claimed in the trail guide. Either ford with your car or on foot. Keep a sharp eye out for a small, crudely painted sign indicating the way to the falls. Park here, if you haven't already, and follow the blazes painted on the trees. You'll have to ford another stream along the footpath, so wear proper footwear or be prepared to go barefoot when the water is high.

The falls are nestled in heavy woods. You're almost upon them before you see them. Assuming you aren't foolish enough to go during hunting season, you'll appreciate the tranquility and solitude.

For those who are not so adventurous, **Tallulah Falls** can be surveyed from several overlooks on US 23/441 south of Clayton. A scenic loop off the main road presents a spectacular vista. A privately owned park with an easygoing hiking trail and Lovers Leap observation deck exhibit a closer look for a small fee. The rugged gorge through which the river tumbles is impressive.

Toccoa Falls is located on the grounds of Toccoa College on State 17. You can drive almost to the base; then a short walk on a level, paved path leads you to the base of a long, straight plunge of 186 feet from above. There is a small admission charge to the falls. A gift shop and restrooms are available.

Keown Falls, Armuchee District, is reached by Forest Service Road 202. A 1.8-mile loop trail leads to the falls, which can also be reached by using the 3.5-mile Johns Mountain Trail.

At **Cloudland Canyon,** a state park in extreme North-west Georgia, Daniel Creek and Bear Creek have gouged out deep canyons through which they rush and plummet. When the two streams meet, they form Sitton Gulch Creek, which courses 900 feet below the canyon's lip. Trails and overlooks afford magnificent vistas of several falls, jagged ravines, and promontories. On the Waterfall Trail, wooden walkways lead to both the 50-foot upper falls and the 100-foot lower falls. A round-trip to both covers about a mile. The park also features the 4.9-mile West Rim Loop Trail and the 5.4-mile Cloudland Backcountry Trail, which requires a permit and a small fee for overnight backpacking, but not for day use.

A one-mile trail from Forest Service Road 283 leads to five cascades at **High Shoals**. Other waterfalls to explore in North Georgia include three separate falls at **DeSoto Falls, Holcomb Creek,** and **Ammon Creek Falls, Minnehaha Falls**, a series of cascades at **Panther Creek, Angel Falls, Clay Creek Falls, Jacks River Falls, Raven Cliff Falls, Nancytown Falls,** and a small cascade at **Barnes Creek**. Believe it or not, there are even more.

You can enjoy waterfalls at all times of year. Spring usual-ly finds the greatest water flow as well as brilliant flowering bushes and trees. Azaleas and dogwoods abound in the early spring, followed by a profusion of rhododendrons and laurels in late spring.

In summer, cool shadows, formed by thick canopies of trees, are a welcome relief from the heat of lower elevations. Wildflowers paint the hillsides. Fall is resplendent with a bright palette of colored leaves. Even winter can be attrac-tive. Stark branches are etched against the sky, and crowds are blessedly absent. Any time, you'll survey myriad species of trees and a variety of wildlife.

North Georgia teems with stunning waterfalls, but their

enticing beauty can be fatal, so Rule 3 is: Don't try to climb rocks around waterfalls or go close to the edge of the rapids. Rocks are covered with slippery lichens that can cause you to fall. Several of Georgia's waterfalls have a 50 to 100 percent death rate for those who have fallen over. Observation decks have been built at the most popular falls—use them.

Here are the rest of our hiking rules:

4. Wear comfortable clothes and shoes or hiking boots and take an extra pair of dry socks and a sweater along.

5. There are very few restrooms or porta-potties except in the large parks, so plan accordingly.

6. Take your camera and lots of film. Binoculars are good, too. As mentioned, a backpack or fannypack is best for carrying.

7. Avoid holidays. If you have no choice, pick less popular falls to visit.

8. Don't go alone, and always let someone know where you are.

9. Stay on the trails, and don't try to cut out switchbacks.

10. Beware of hypothermia in cool weather. If you are cold, wet, and exhausted, take measures to dry off and warm up immediately.

11. Don't leave a trace of your passing either by littering or picking foliage.

12. Get a good Forest Service map or a set of U.S. Geologic Survey Maps for the area you will be exploring. The best guide we have found is "The Trail Guide to the Chattahoochee-Oconee National Forests," available from the U.S. Forest Service.

13. Most important: have fun.

Most of North Georgia's trails are blazed. Standard practice is for a single blaze to mark a trail and a double blaze to indicate an abrupt or confusing turn.

IMPORTANT TRAILS IN GEORGIA

The Appalachian, Benton MacKaye, Bartram, and Duncan Ridge Trails are all, or in part, located within the Chattahoochee National Forest in the mountains of North Georgia. (For information on these trails, see the addresses and phone numbers on page 79.) The Pine Mountain Trail is next to Franklin D. Roosevelt State Park in West Central Georgia.

Appalachian Trail

Because of its national renown, the Appalachian Trail is the most-hiked trail in Georgia. The southern terminus of the 2,000-mile trail is located at Springer Mountain in North Georgia. The seventy-nine-mile section in Georgia stretches from there to Bly Gap on the North Carolina border.

In addition to the two endpoints, you can approach the trail from Amicalola Falls State Park, Blood Mountain Spur Trail, or Logan Turnpike Trail. You can access different sections of the trail from Woody Gap, Neels Gap, Hogpen Gap, Unicoi Gap, and Dicks Creek Gap. Volunteers maintain the trail.

In addition to the Forest Service, you can contact:

Georgia Appalachian Trail Club, Inc.
P.O. Box 654
Atlanta, GA 30301

Benton MacKaye Trail

Benton MacKaye was the forester who envisioned the Appalachian Trail. He also conceived a need for loop trails that would provide access to as well as offer alternative trails to the much-used Appalachian Trail. The 250-mile MacKaye Trail runs, in part, along the western edge of the Blue Ridge Mountains where MacKaye himself initially envisioned the Appalachian Trail. The MacKaye Trail intersects the Appalachian Trail at three points, forming a huge figure-eight trail system in the mountainous regions of Georgia, Tennessee, and North Carolina.

The Benton MacKaye Trail shares with the Appalachian Trail its southern terminus on Springer Mountain and includes the Cohutta Wilderness. It also merges at times with the Duncan Ridge Trail. The Benton MacKaye Trail, in Georgia, stretches fifty miles from Springer Mountain to Double Spring Gap on the Tennessee border on the eastern side of the Cohutta Wilderness, most of it within the Chattahoochee National Forest. It varies in elevation from 1,500 feet to 3,600 feet. Terrain varies from streamside walking paths to scenic ridgetops. Major attractions include Long Creek Falls and Fall Branch Falls as well as a 250-foot hiker's suspension bridge across the Toccoa River. Remote and primitive, the trail provides no shelters. However, parking is available at all access points.

The Benton MacKaye Trail Association was organized in 1980 to build and maintain the trail in conjunction with the U.S. Forest Service. The association holds monthly trail construction and maintenance outings. Memberships and eight detailed maps of the trail sections are available. In addition to the Forest Service, you can contact:

Benton MacKaye Trail Association
P.O. Box 53271
Atlanta, GA 30355-1271

William Bartram Trail

This National Recreation Trail in the Tallulah Ranger District is named for an eighteenth-century explorer and naturalist who traveled over 900 miles throughout the wilds of the infant state. The trail traces his route for thirty-seven miles from the Georgia/North Carolina border over the summit of Rabun Bald to the Chattooga River. Of the four major trails in North Georgia, this is the least taxing. For more information, contact the Forest Service.

Duncan Ridge Trail

This challenging trail follows ridges for 30.5 miles, which is most of its length. It is divided into two sections. The first section begins at Long Creek near Three Forks and extends 10.5 miles to State 60. Section II climbs 20.4 miles from there to Slaughter Gap. This section is considered the most strenuous long segment of trail in Georgia. At times the trail merges with the Appalachian and/or Benton MacKaye Trails. Contact the Forest Service for more information.

Pine Mountain Trail

Descending from the lofty heights of the North Georgia mountains doesn't mean you have to forgo challenging hiking. In 1975, volunteers of the Pine Mountain Trail Association built the twenty-three-mile footpath crossing and following the

Pine Mountain Ridge in West Central Georgia, which they continue to maintain. Much of the land once belonged to Franklin D. Roosevelt. The trail covers tranquil woods, bubbling streams, frothy waterfalls, rock outcroppings, abundant wildflowers, and lush foliage. There are few steep, tiring grades. Scenic overlooks unfold clear views of distant ridges.

The trail extends from the F.D.R. State Park entrance near the Callaway Gardens Country Store to the town of Warm Springs, where President Roosevelt had his Little White House. The trail is used by 40,000 hikers annually. Amenities include nine designated campsites—all near water.

You can purchase memberships in the association as well as inexpensive maps and patches. Maps are also available at the F.D.R. State Park Welcome Center. Contact:

Pine Mountain Trail Association, Inc.
c/o Wickham's Outdoor World, Inc.
Cross Country Plaza
Columbus, GA 31906

HIKING IN THE CHATTAHOOCHEE
AND OCONEE NATIONAL FORESTS

The two national forests, which occupy an enormous part of the state (almost one million acres), offer numerous recreation areas with good hiking trails ranging from easy to difficult. The vast majority of those trails are one to two miles long. Some recreation areas are open only part of the year. However, you can still hike the trail in the off-season if you're willing to walk to the trailheads. The trails we'll describe are listed with the appropriate ranger station to contact if you want more information. Their addresses and phone numbers are listed at the end of this section.

Brasstown Bald, Brasstown Ranger District

From atop the highest mountain in Georgia (elevation 4,784 feet), you can get a 360-degree vista of Georgia, Tennessee, and South Carolina. A steep drive up the mountain brings you to the parking area and a Welcome Center/gift shop. You have two choices to get to the summit. If you're physically fit, you can (and should) walk. Although the trail is only one-quarter-mile long, it is steep. However, the path is paved, and there are several resting spots along the way. The other alternative is a shuttle bus, which is available for a small fee.

At the apex, you can admire the view and then stop at the Visitor Center to see interpretive displays and a slide program. Rangers are on duty to answer your questions.

In addition to the Trail to Summit, the parking lot opens onto the 5.4-mile Arkaquah Trail and the 4.5-mile Jacks Knob Trail, both considered strenuous. The mountain is located in North Georgia off the State 180 spur between Blairsville and Cleveland.

Pocket Recreation Area, Armuchee Ranger District

This area gets its name because it lies in a low area surrounded on three sides by the steep ridges of Horn Mountain. The 2.5-mile trail follows low-lying streambeds. You may spot deer in isolated coves or along ridges.

HIKING AND ARCHAEOLOGY
IN THE NATIONAL FORESTS

Amateur archaeologists can combine hiking with examining the past. **Track Rock Archeological Area, Brasstown District,** features preserved petroglyphs of ancient Indian origin. The carvings resemble animal and bird tracks, human footprints, crosses, and circles. Near Blairsville, the area has no facilities.

Scull Shoals Historical Area, Oconee District, in Central Georgia, contains the remains of a once-prosperous town, the site of Georgia's first paper mill as well as an early cotton gin and textile factory. You can reach the area by road or by hiking a one-mile trail. From there, you can take the short, easy **Boarding House Trail** through flat, piney woods to the remains of a historic boarding house. **Indian Mounds Trail** traverses the Oconee River floodplain to two prehistoric mounds.

WILDERNESS AREAS IN THE NATIONAL FORESTS

In addition to the more developed scenic and recreation areas, the Chattahoochee-Oconee National Forests contain several wilderness areas.

Cohutta Wilderness, Cohutta District, a 34,100-acre wilderness that sits astride the Georgia/Tennessee border, contains the rugged southern end of the Appalachian Mountain Chain. A network of trails provides ideal hiking for the backpacker and hardy outdoor person. Access to the interior is by footpath only.

Two of the best trout streams in the state are within the wilderness boundary. Bear, feral hogs, and white-tailed deer are among the species occupying the isolated forest. Exercise special caution around the rivers, which can be dangerous in periods of high water following a storm.

The **Chattooga Wild and Scenic River, Tallulah District,** is one of the longest free-flowing rivers in the Southeast. Still relatively primitive and undeveloped, it is used mostly for white-water rafting and kayaking, but also for fishing and hiking.

Ellicott's Rock Wilderness, Tallulah District, straddles three states: Georgia and both Carolinas. The cornerstone where they meet was named after the surveyor of the thirty-fifth parallel.

Southern Nantahala Wilderness, Brasstown and Tallulah Districts, sprawls across the Georgia/North Carolina border. This area has no conveniences, so visitors must be totally self-sufficient. Access is by foot or horseback.

Raven Cliffs Trail is in the newly developed **Raven Cliffs Wilderness Area**. The trail follows cascading Dodd Creek 2.5 miles upstream to the cliffs.

Special Trails in the National Forest

Sosebee Cove Trail, Brasstown Ranger District, circles through one of the finest stands of second-growth hardwood in the country and is also noted for the variety of wildflowers.

Lakeshore Trail, Chestatee Ranger District, encircles Dockery Lake and is accessible to the handicapped.

Signs along the **Warwoman Dell Nature Trail, Tallulah Ranger District,** identify many common plants and their relationships in the ecosystem.

Trails with particularly good views: **Ladyslipper, Panther Creek, Dockery Lake, Raven Rocks,** and **Lake Blue Ridge.**

Trails limited to foot travel only: **Chickamauga Creek** and **Taylors Ridge.**

Trails for novice hikers: **Bear Hair, Horse Trough Falls, Broad River, Sourwood, Twin Bridges,** and others.

Trails longer than five miles: **Appalachian, Bartram, Benton Mackaye, Duncan Ridge, Chickamauga** (6.2 miles), **Arkaquah** (5.5 miles), **Coosa** (12.7 miles), **Lady-slipper** (6.2 miles), **Panther Creek** (5.5 miles), **Mountaintown** (5.6 miles), **Windy Gap** (5 miles), **Chattooga** (10.7 miles), **Three Forks** (9.5 miles), and **Rich Mountain** (8.8 miles).

Trails with difficult segments: **Arkaquah, Brasstown Bald, Byron Herbert Reece, Anna Ruby Falls, Dukes Creek, Panther Creek, DeSoto Falls, Logan Turnpike, Mountaintown Creek, Three Forks,** and **Rich Mountain.**

Trails that access the Appalachian Trail: **Byron Herbert Reece, Jacks Knob, Jarrard Gap, Slaughter Creek, Andrews Cove, Logan Turnpike,** and **Dockery Lake.**

The **Coosa Backcountry Trail** requires a permit, which you can obtain free at the Vogel State Park Visitor Center. This 12.7-mile loop trail is of moderate to strenuous difficulty.

The U.S. Forest Service puts out two helpful brochures. "Directory—Chattahoochee-Oconee National Forests Recreation Areas" describes each area, how to get there, and its special features. "Trail Guide to the Chattahoochee-Oconee National Forests" contains maps and a detailed description of sixty-three trails and how to get to them. For either guide, contact:

Forest Supervisor
U.S. Forest Service
508 Oak Street, N.W.

Gainesville, GA 30501
404-536-0541

You may also contact any of the Chattahoochee-Oconee
National Forest Ranger Districts:

Armuchee
P.O. Box 465
LaFayette, GA 30728
706-638-1085

Cohutta
401 Old Ellijay Road
Chatsworth, GA 30705
706-695-6736

Brasstown
US 19/129 S.
Box 216
Blairsville, GA 30512
706-745-6928

Oconee
349 Forsyth Street
Monticello, GA 31064
912-468-2244

Tallulah
Chechero/Savannah Street
P.O. Box 438
Clayton, GA 30525
706-632-3031

Chattooga
P.O. Box 196, Burton Road
Clarkesville, GA 30523
706-754-6221

Chestatee
200 West Main Street
P.O. Box 2080
Dahlonega, GA 30533
706-864-6173

Toccoa
Suite 5, Owenby Building
East Main Street
Blue Ridge, GA 30513
706-632-3031

HIKING IN STATE PARKS AND HISTORIC SITES

Georgia State Parks and Historic Sites
1352 Floyd Tower East

205 Butler Street, S.E.
Atlanta, GA 30334
404-656-3530
800-342-7275 in Georgia
800-542-7275 outside Georgia

Every state park and historic site in Georgia has designated hiking trails with backcountry trails as long as thirteen miles. Some trails hook up with others, giving you infinite hiking possibilities.

State parks with outstanding hiking trails include **Black Rock Mountain, Cloudland Canyon, Franklin D. Roosevelt, Fort Mountain, Providence Canyon, Unicoi,** and **Vogel.** Several parks were also mentioned in the Waterfalls section.

Shorter nature trails focus on specific animal and plant habitats and geologic features. Some trails of special interest can be found at **Amicalola Falls, Elijah Clark, George T. Bagby, High Falls, Panola Mountain, Reed Bingham, Seminole, Stephen C. Foster, Sweetwater Creek, Tugaloo,** and **Vogel State Parks.**

Providence Canyon

Known as Georgia's "Little Grand Canyon," this spectacular natural wonder is the result of only 100 years of erosion. Slender solitary rock formations jutting up from the canyon floor create the illusion of being out West. Varicolored ravine walls create an attractive natural painting. In addition to spectacular panoramas, the park has the highest concentration of wildflowers in the state as well as a large number of plumleaf azaleas, which are found only within a 100-mile radius. In addition to three miles of hiking trails and six miles of backpacking trails, the park features an Interpretive Center, picnic areas, pioneer camps, and a group shelter. Call 912-838-6202 for information.

HIKING IN AND AROUND METRO ATLANTA

Chattahoochee River National Recreation Area
1978 Island Ford Parkway
Dunwoody, GA 30350
404-399-8070 or 404-952-4419

You don't have to travel miles from the city to find good hiking. The Chattahoochee River National Recreation Area snakes through the metro Atlanta area, providing forty-eight miles of recreational opportunities. Units of the park in the Atlanta area are Suwanee Creek and Abbotts Bridge near Duluth, Medlock Bridge and Jones Bridge near Alpharetta, Vickery Creek in Roswell, Island Ford and Gold Branch near Dunwoody, and Johnson Ferry, Cochran Shoals, Palisades, and Paces Mill near Marietta.

Upland ridge trails in the **Palisades Unit** lead to panoramas of the river gorge, floodplains, rock outcroppings, sandy beaches, and expanses of shoal water.

The **Cochran Fitness Trail**, approximately three miles long with optional loops, is an activity path with twenty-two exercise stations.

To tell or not to tell, that is our question about the **Vickery Creek Unit** of the park. For the fourteen years we've lived in Roswell—one of the northern suburbs of Atlanta—this 254-acre park has been almost like our own private hiking ground. We'd hate for it to be "discovered" and ruined by overcrowding.

81

In the heavily wooded forest, an oasis hidden away within the city limits, you can choose from among 11.5 miles of easy, moderate, and difficult trails, including steep bluffs and rock outcroppings. The park offers fishing, rock climbing, and mountain biking as well as a picnic area. You can also explore the historic remains of an 1860s dam built to provide water power for woolen mills.

Kennesaw Mountain National Battlefield Park
900 Kennesaw Mountain Drive
Kennesaw, GA 30144
404-427-4686

In June 1864, Union Gen. William Tecumseh Sherman's advance toward Atlanta was delayed for two weeks at Kennesaw Mountain by Confederate Gen. Joseph E. Johnston, whose troops were entrenched along the ridgetops of Big and Little Kennesaw Mountains, blocking Union movement. After several unsuccessful attempts to dislodge the Confederates, Sherman returned to his previously successful flanking maneuvers and continued his drive toward Atlanta.

The 2,884-acre National Park preserves the battleground and strong earthwork trenches. Sixteen miles of hiking trails crisscross the park. You can get a spectacular view of the Atlanta skyline from the top of the mountain, and on a clear day you can also see Stone Mountain. The hike up the mountain, while paved, is steep. A free shuttle bus offers an alternative method of getting to the top. It operates on the half hour starting at 9:30 A.M. Pets are permitted on the trails if leashed.

Along the trails are troop movement maps, monuments, historical markers, and cannon emplacements. Special living-history programs are presented periodically. A visitors center at the bottom of the mountain features an orientation program, exhibits, and a bookstore. Picnicking areas are available, but there are no overnight facilities.

An excellent resource to hiking in the metropolitan area is *Atlanta Walks* by Ren and Helen Davis (Peachtree Publishers Ltd., 1993). They describe short walks through in-town and near-town parks, historic neighborhoods, colleges and universities, and even a historic cemetery.

HIKING GEORGIA'S CANALS

Two important canals were built in Georgia during the 1800s. The canal at the Okefenokee Swamp was abandoned before it was completed, but it still provides recreational opportunities. The Augusta Canal is still in use.

Canal Diggers Trail
Okefenokee Swamp National Wildlife Refuge
U.S. Fish and Wildlife Service
Okefenokee National Wildlife Refuge
Route 2, Box 338
Folkston, GA 31537
912-496-3331

During the late nineteenth century an attempt was made to drain the gigantic swamp. The Suwannee Canal Company expected to profit from the sale of timber and from croplands exposed by the drainage.

The plan called for the swamp to be drained through Trail Ridge to the Atlantic Ocean by way of the St. Mary's River. However, the canal was never cut down to the water level of the swamp because the diggings exposed springs that created a flow of water back into the swamp. The project was abandoned after only fourteen miles were completed.

While hiking along the sides of the canal, you can see migrating warblers, white-throated sparrows, and other birds during the fall and winter, as well as the gopher tortoise, snakes, raccoons, opossums, foxes, skunks, and armadillos. Dense growths of mosses and ferns line the wet ditch bottoms. In addition, you can hike on the Peckerwood Trail, the Deer Stand Trail, and along a 4,000-foot scenic boardwalk that leads to a fifty-foot observation tower from which you can survey a 360-degree panorama of swamp forests and prairies.

Augusta Canal
Augusta Canal Authority
801 Broad Street, Room 507
Augusta, GA 30901
706-722-1071

The nine-mile Augusta Canal is a National Historic Landmark. Today, just as when it opened in 1846, the canal provides industrial and recreational uses. The canal is being restored and refurbished so that it and the landmark buildings along it will be preserved.

The old towpath, where mules towed barges up and down the canal, follows the entire length either along the inland side or the land separation between the canal and the Savannah River. This path provides excellent hiking.

A levee, separate from the canal bank, runs seven miles along the canal. Part of it is incorporated into the Riverwalk Park for easy strolling. You can also amble around Lakes Warren and Olmstead, which are connected to the canal.

The distance from the dam to I-20 is 2.05 miles; from the dam to the pumping station, 3.5 miles; from the dam to 13th Street, 7.0 miles; and from the dam to Riverwalk, 8.5 miles.

In 1773, naturalist William Bartram explored along the river. You can see many of the same plants and animals he recorded.

HIKING ON GEORGIA'S BARRIER ISLANDS

Golden Isles Tourist & Convention Bureau
4 Glynn Avenue
Brunswick, GA 31520
912-265-0620

Georgia's barrier islands—Tybee, Skidaway, Wassaw, Ossabaw, St. Catherine's, Blackbeard, Sapelo, Wolf, Little St. Simons, St. Simons, Jekyll, and Cumberland—are collectively known as the Golden Isles. Individually, they provide hiking on miles of wide, hard-packed, unspoiled beach as well as through forests of slash pine, palmetto, holly, Southern magnolia, and live oak dripping with Spanish moss. **Jekyll Island**, for example, provides twenty miles of hiking/biking trails.

Some of the islands are densely populated; others, such as Little St. Simons and Cumberland, are scarcely inhabited. Several islands are either all or in part wildlife refuges or wildlife management areas. Wildlife sanctuaries include **Wassaw Island National Wildlife Refuge, Ossabaw Island and Heritage Preserve, Blackbeard Wilderness Area and National Wildlife Refuge, R.J. Reynolds Wildlife Management Area, Sapelo Island National Estuarine Area and Sanctuary,** and **Wolf Island National Wildlife Refuge.**

NATIONAL WILDLIFE REFUGES

Department of the Interior
U.S. Fish and Wildlife Service
Richard B. Russell Federal Building
75 Spring Street, S.W.
Atlanta, GA 30303
404-331-0295

Little St. Simons Island
P.O. Box 1078
St. Simons, GA 31522
912-638-7472
Contact: Deborah McIntyre

This privately owned island is accessible only by a twice-daily private ferry. However, the 10,000-acre island is opened to overnight guests during certain periods of the year. Little St. Simons caters to a maximum of twenty-four guests at a time. On-staff naturalists guide guests on scheduled and private hikes through pristine forests, freshwater ponds, isolated beaches, and marshlands where they are likely to catch glimpses of freely roaming deer, alligators, armadillos, and snakes as well as over 200 species of birds, including soaring eagles, egrets, wood stork, heron, and red-winged blackbirds. When we visited the island, we were so enchanted with the deer that we started photographing them. After burning up several rolls of film, we realized that the deer were plentiful. We got so blasé that we began to say, "Oh, another deer. Oh well." Guests to the island often participate in a deer or turtle nest count.

Cumberland Island Wilderness Area
and National Seashore
National Park Service
P.O. Box 806
St. Marys, GA 31558
912-882-4337

Twenty miles of beach seem to stretch out endlessly. Inland miles of sand-and-crushed-shell roads wander through ancient maritime forests. Wildlife you're likely to see includes birds, alligators, deer, wild horses, and sea turtles. The only access to the island is by National Park Service ferry. Campers and day-trippers are strictly limited to 300 per day. You must have reservations for the ferry and/or camping.

GUIDES/OUTFITTERS

Mountain Crossings at Walasi-yi is a historic site where the Appalachian Trail crosses US 19/129 at Neels Gap north of Dahlonega. The center is a complete backpacking outfitter. Call 706-745-6095 for information.

Georgia Mountain Adventures & Creations offers half- and full-day scenic mountain and waterfalls hiking with shuttle service. Call 706-878-1263 for information.

Georgia Wildlife Adventures, 404-978-0624, is operated by Tim Zech. All you have to do is tell him where you want to go and he'll customize a plan for you. The services of Georgia Wildlife Adventures are particularly popular with out-of-towners. Tim will pick you up at your hotel, transport you to the desired location, provide all equipment and accessories, and return you to the hotel at the end of the day.

Real Rabun
Route 1, Box 242
Tiger, GA 30576
706-782-5014

These all-day guided hiking trips provide glimpses of off-the-beaten-track areas. The service includes a shuttle, vehicle storage, and a picnic lunch.

Rabun County Welcome Center
US 441 North
Clayton, GA 30525
706-782-4812

At this center, you can pick up hiking maps and peruse an extensive file of hiking trails. Some other good places to go for gear and/or advice are:

High Country Outfitters
Rio at Midtown, Suite D203-1
595 Piedmont Avenue
Atlanta, GA 30308
404-892-0909

REI
1800 NE Expressway
Atlanta, GA 30329
404-633-6508

Call of the Wild
425 Market Place
Roswell, GA 30075
404-992-5400

Bibliography

Davis, Ren and Helen. *Atlanta Walks.* Atlanta: Peachtree Publishers, Inc., 1993.

Homan, Tim. *The Hiking Trails of North Georgia.* Atlanta: Peachtree Publishers, Ltd., 1987.

5HORSEBACK RIDING

Many girls go through a horse-loving stage during their middle-school years. Never having satisfied that longing, Carol is always eager to head on out for a trail ride at every vacation destination. Dan is resigned to, but certainly not thrilled about, tagging along. When you consider that she's eager and he's not, it's a mystery how often Carol gets matched up with the Horse from Hell while Dan serenely plods along on a perfectly behaved animal.

We're not the only enthusiasts of touring on horseback. Today many people feel that the best way to enjoy Georgia's mountains, wildflowers, wildlife, babbling brooks, rushing streams and rivers, plunging waterfalls, sandy beaches, and sounds of nature is astride a horse. Georgia offers a wide variety of horseback riding experiences for riders of all experience levels. That's only as it should be. After all, so it's claimed, people have been riding horses in Georgia since

Hernando de Soto came through about 1540. It's thought that he brought the first horses to the state and may have left a few with the Cherokee Indians.

OVERNIGHT TRAIL RIDES

F.D.R. Riding Stables
Franklin D. Roosevelt State Park
Box 2970, State 190 East
Pine Mountain, GA 31822
706-628-4533

Long before the movie *City Slickers* came out, overnight horseback riding trips complete with chuckwagon and all-night campfires were providing an Old West experience for modern-day cowpokes at the **Stables at Franklin D. Roosevelt State Park** near Pine Mountain in the Presidential Pathways region of Southwest Georgia. This riding/camping experience is ideal for families, but it is equally popular with adults-only groups, and it is becoming increasingly accepted as a business junket.

Our experience in joining a group of five families on one of these campouts was a typical one. Riders ranged from seven years old to fiftysomething and came from all levels of riding experience. Our group of twenty was accompanied by three cowboys.

We intrepid adventurers left the stables about 4:00 P.M. and rode about 2.5 hours through deep woods to the camping site atop Pine Mountain. (Horseback riding is not permitted on the Pine Mountain Trail.) The trail is barely wide enough for a horse to pass between the trees. Add our legs on either side, and we were in for some very tight squeezes.

91

This is not a flat path that any old nag can slog along. There are rivers and streams to ford and some very steep hills to ascend and descend. Low-hanging branches lie in wait to steal your hat. You'll know you've had an adventure, not an afternoon stroll. Along the trail you're likely to see deer, wild turkeys, and even bobcats.

Once at the campsite, we participated in unsaddling and brushing the horses as well as setting up camp, tending the fire, and preparing meals. The staff set up an authentic chuck-wagon filled with metal dishes, utensils, and pots and pans. Many one-pot meals can be cooked over the open fire, but in addition there are several grills if steak, hamburgers, or hot dogs are more what you have in mind.

After dinner, we relaxed around the blazing fire singing, swapping lies, telling ghost stories, and gorging on S'mores until the wee hours. Then we turned in for a short night's sleep. Some diehards chose to sleep by the campfire, while we and others opted for communal living in a large Army tent floored with straw.

Morning came all too soon and with it some mighty sore muscles and creaking bones. After breakfast horses were saddled up and we got underway for the one-hour return trip to the stables. The trail back is not as difficult as the outbound track—it's less steep, crosses some open meadows, and skirts a tranquil lake.

You need to bring your own sleeping bag. Depending on the package you've chosen, you may bring your own food or it may be included. Sleeping bags, equipment, and food are transported to the campsite by truck.

Although the stables offer overnight trips of up to five nights, owner Wayne Wilkins suggests a one-nighter for the inexperienced. We strongly agree. We would have taken on a lot more than we could handle if we'd tried for a longer excursion.

If you want a less strenuous experience, choose one of the shorter trail rides ranging from an hour to half a day. From the stables, you can explore the beauty of the 12,000-acre park on horseback along sixty miles of scenic trails that wind through acreage given to the United States by the Creek Indians under the famous Indian Springs Treaty of 1825. Well-traveled visitors compare the scenery and the trail riding experience favorably to that of Colorado and Wyoming. The park is named for President Roosevelt, who had his Little White House nearby at Warm Springs, where he went for the therapeutic waters.

The most popular ride is the one-hour excursion along the Bridle Trail. It follows a gurgling mountain stream where it's not unusual to see various wildlife in their natural settings.

The two- to three-hour Thoroughbred Trail ride takes riders to the top of Pine Mountain for a breathtaking view of the valley and Lake Franklin.

For the more dauntless rider, the four- to five-hour ride along the Buffalo Trail is a must. Horsemen often leave the trails and have to depend on a compass. This is the only trail where running the horses is allowed.

Another popular ride includes an afternoon cookout. Wayne can't help bragging that his baked beans are famous. We can't ever remember meeting a man who loved his work as much as Wayne does. An escapee from corporate life, he chucked it all to ride the range, so to speak. He does everything—takes reservations, accompanies the rides, feeds the animals, even assists at livestock births.

He's created a true farm/ranch atmosphere at the stable, enhanced by a collection of cows, chickens, goats, and pigs, most of which wander around loose, allowing many children their first opportunity to see a farm animal up close and personal. These gentle creatures are tame and friendly; they all have names and most answer to them.

A big hit right now is Wilma, a huge, pot-bellied pig who will allow herself to be saddled and ridden by small children, much to their delight. You can't tell who's squealing louder—the kids or the pig. Another pig will sit on command for a cookie.

Doc is an affable calf who often sleeps on the floor in Wayne's office, as if he were a pet dog, and has even been known to ride in the front seat of Wayne's truck and feast on ice cream from a local drive-through. The last time we were there, two adorable orphaned calves had been added to the menagerie. They were bottle-fed by the visiting children, and they were insatiable.

Albert is the one star attraction you can't get to close to—he's a papered true American buffalo.

The stables are open 365 days a year. Even during the winter months, the welcome mat is out. A campfire is kept going in the stable yard all day, always with a pot of fresh coffee brewing. Surprisingly, the busiest day of the year is Thanksgiving. Undoubtedly, the most festive evening for an overnight trip is New Year's Eve. Wayne tells us that from the crest of the mountain, you can get a spectacular view of all the fireworks being set off in the valley.

Make reservations for busy times as early as you can. All the overnights fill up fast. Rates are seasonal; lower rates are in effect during the winter season, from the third week of September through the last week of May.

All rides are accompanied by experienced trail guides. Thirty-five well-trained horses are kept at the stables, assuring that each rider can be matched to the horse that's right for him. On our expedition, my horse and I had a personality conflict, but no problem—I just traded horses with one of the guides. Other horses can be supplied for very large groups with advance notice.

Children from six months to four years old can ride if they share the horse with a parent. Parents have the option of riding with a four- to seven-year-old, or the child may ride alone. Children eight and above ride alone.

Overnights can be arranged on the weekends or during the week. Ask about group rates, carriage rides, old-fashioned hayrides, cow cutting, putting up fencing, and other recreations of life in the Old West. Just about any activity can be customized for your group.

Eagle Adventure Company
P.O. Box 970
McCaysville, GA 30555
800-288-3245

Eagle Adventure Company is located in McCaysville, in the mountains on the Georgia/Tennessee/North Carolina border, with many of its activities actually taking place outside the state of Georgia.

The two-day guided trail ride covers twenty miles across the Unicoi Gap. Tennessee walking horses—ideal for children and first-time riders—are used across the rough terrain. Overnights are only scheduled for several fall weekends but can be arranged at other times for groups.

A three-day "Ranch, Raft and Rail" package includes horseback riding in the Cherokee National Forest, whitewater rafting on the Ocoee River, and a train ride on the

Great Smoky Mountain Railway through the Nantahala River Gorge. Accommodations for this package are in rustic bunkhouses, cabins, or bed and breakfasts.

RIDING ALONG GEORGIA'S COAST

Riding horseback on the beach was one of our longtime romantic dreams. That fantasy was finally fulfilled a couple of years ago in Bermuda. Had we only done some research, we would have discovered that the opportunity was awaiting us much closer to home. You can ride on the beach at both Sea Island and Little St. Simons Island.

Sea Island Stables
Box 281
Sea Island, GA 31561
912-638-1032
Contact: Marvin Long, Manager; Amy Long Kutrufis, Assistant Manager

Located smack in the middle of the sparkling upscale development of homes and hotels on swanky Sea Island is the farmlike Sea Island Stables. In operation since 1948, the stable is operated as a concession of the five-star, five-diamond Cloister Resort but is also open to the public.

The stable offers rides along the marsh or to a private beach at the southern end of island. In the summer there's a special treat: a swim with your horse where you ride bareback into the water. In good weather, picnic rides are featured on Tuesday and Saturday. Both English and western saddles are available. To participate in these rides, you must be able to control your horse at a trot.

Open every day except Christmas morning, the stable also provides lessons in English riding and stabling if you have brought your own horse. Children enjoy the farm animals freely roaming around the stable yard. When we visited, a group of seven-year-olds were celebrating a birthday party with riding in the ring, games, and a cookout.

Little St. Simons Island
P.O. Box 1078
St. Simons, GA 31522
912-638-7472
Contact: Deborah McIntyre

I'm here to tell you that Elvis *is* dead—no matter what the tabloids say. We were horseback riding on this private island (the Berolzheimer family uses the island much of the year, but there are certain periods when it is open to overnight guests), and I was teamed up with a horse named Elvis.

This horse has so absorbed the laid-back atmosphere of the island, he sees no reason to move faster than a slow stroll, no matter what his rider might want. As a result, we were continually holding everyone else up while Elvis stopped to munch Spanish moss dripping from the low-hanging branches or casually survey his domain.

Little St. Simons lies adjacent to heavily developed St. Simons and is accessible only by a twice-daily private ferry. The 10,000-acre island caters to a maximum of twenty-four guests at a time with a staff of seventeen, including two full-time naturalists and an intern, a stable manager, fishing and boating guides, and an outstanding kitchen staff. Horseback riding is offered in the morning and the afternoon.

A SPECIAL PLACE

Wills Park Equestrian Center
11915 Wills Road
Alpharetta, GA 30201
404-740-2400

A branch of the Fulton County Park System, Wills Park hosts numerous equestrian events. The facility includes outdoor and covered rings as well as numerous stalls for visiting horses. Many equestrians also practice here.

Equestrian Paths

Chickamauga and Chattanooga National Military Park
US 27
Ft. Oglethorpe, GA 30742
706-866-9241
Contact: Dan Brown, Superintendent

The battlefield straddles the Georgia/Tennessee border. The Georgia side of the park was the site of one of the most decisive Confederate victories of the Civil War. Explore the woods and meadows much as a cavalry soldier might have done, albeit more peacefully. Admire the monuments and read the historic markers explaining the battle. The park provides seven to twelve miles of marked trails for horseback riding with a designated area for parking horse trailers.

Hitching posts are available in the parking area. The park is open all year except Christmas. Admission is free. Proof of a negative Coggins test is required for every horse entering these areas. It is best to call ahead and make arrangements before visiting.

Chattahoochee-Oconee National Forest
Tallulah Ranger District
Chechero/Savannah Street
P.O. Box 438
Clayton, GA 30525
706-782-3320

Open all year, the **Willis Knob Trail** in Georgia and the Rocky Gap Trail in South Carolina combine to offer 27.5 miles of scenic horseback riding in the southern Blue Ridge mountains. The Willis Knob Trail spans a large, fifteen-mile continuous loop, while the Rocky Gap Trail has several loops and is 12.5 miles long. Each trail is crossed by several gravel roads, allowing you to plan trips from .5 mile to the full 27.5 miles. Campsites, toilet facilities, twenty stalls, and a spring-fed watering trough are available at the **Willis Knob Group Horse Camp**. Each site has a cooking grill, a picnic table, and a lantern post. Reservations are required, and there is a non-refundable reservation fee and a one-night user fee.

In the Chattahoochee National Forest, **Ladyslipper Trail** winds 6.2 miles up and down hillsides through wooded areas and offers several scenic panoramas.

In the Oconee National Forest, the **Burgess Mountain Trail** meanders one mile to the highest point in the forest: 645 feet. **Kinnard Creek Trail** traverses 4.1 miles of piney woods and bottoms from **Concord Hunt Camp** to **Horse**

Hunt Camp. Two trails follow the Ocmulgee River. **Wise Creek Trail** follows the river for 2.5 miles through piney woods and hardwood bottoms. The **Ocmulgee River Trail** follows flat, piney bottoms for 2.8 miles along the river.

Horseback riding is prohibited on the Appalachian Trail and the Bartram Trail in Georgia as well as in some areas of the Cohutta Wilderness.

Chattahoochee River National Recreation Area
1978 Island Ford Parkway
Dunwoody, GA 30350
404-393-7912

This massive park with several sites scattered throughout the metro Atlanta area is open all year except Christmas. Horseback riding is allowed in all units except the Cochran Shoals area.

Hard Labor Creek State Park
Knox Chapel Road
Rutledge, GA 30663
706-557-3001
Contact: Bruce Roper, Manager

The park maintains over seventeen miles of horse trails, providing up to five hours of riding, but does not rent horses. There is a small daily charge for riding. Stalls are available for a small daily fee, which includes the riding charge. Parking for trailers is provided at the stables, as are campsites that include water and electrical hookups for campers and trailers. These sites feature picnic tables as well as comfort stations and hot water. Advance reservations are required.

WILDLIFE MANAGEMENT AREAS

Game and Fish Division
Georgia Department of Natural Resources
205 Butler Street, S.E.
Room 1362
Atlanta, GA 30334
404-656-3522

There are sixty-seven wildlife management areas throughout the state, and horses are allowed in many of them, provided riders adhere to certain rules and regulations. These locations are also sometimes opened to hunters, so it is advisable to check hunting season dates.

OTHER HORSEBACK RIDING FACILITIES

Cohutta Lodge Riding Stables
5000 Cochise Trail
Chatsworth, GA 30705
800-325-6686 outside Georgia
706-695-9601 inside Georgia

Cohutta Lodge offers guided one-hour, two-hour, and half-day mountain trail rides through the Chattahoochee National Forest in Northwest Georgia. The lodge plans to feature overnight trail rides. Camp will already be set up, and guides will provide an all-you-can-eat campfire supper and breakfast.

Horse Outfitters
Dahlonega, GA 30533

706-864-9333
Contact: Bill and Linda Green

Bill and Linda Green offer guided trail rides, overnight camping, and two one-week summer horse camps for boys and girls nine to thirteen. Guides are knowledgeable about horses, wildflowers, and tall tales.

Southeastern Expeditions
2936-H North Druid Hills Road
Atlanta, GA 30329
800-868-RAFT or, in Atlanta, 404-329-0433
Ocoee Outpost, 615-338-8073
Chattooga Outpost, 706-782-4331

Covered in detail in Chapter 9, Southeastern Expeditions offers a unique program, called Saddle & Paddle, which involves horseback riding one day and white-water rafting the next.

Swan's Nest Farm Monastery
Star Route, Box 246
Marble Hill, GA 30148
706-475-0199

Swan's Nest offers basic trail rides for any level of riding experience. A one-hour trail ride follows twenty minutes of instruction in the arena. Custom trail rides can be arranged for more experienced riders. Rides are held Sundays by reservation only.

Other activities at Swan's Nest include summer camp (see below), Christmas and Spring Break programs, Saturday children's and adults' clinics, and private lessons.

**Chattahoochee
Horse Hotel**
Route 2, Box 2357
Clayton, GA 30535
706-782-4385
Contact: Bob and Judy
   Labrozzi

Dillard Horse Stables
Old Dillard Road
Dillard, GA 30537
706-746-5348
Contact: Walt Lane

Gold City Corral
Route 3, Box 510
Dahlonega, GA 30533
706-864-6456
Contact: Frank Kraft

Lake Lanier Islands
6950 Holiday Road
Lake Lanier Islands, GA
   30518
404-945-6701

**Rabun County
Recreation Park**
Clayton, GA 30525
706-782-4600

**Smokey Mountain
Riding Stables**
P.O. Box 149
Wiley, GA 30581
706-782-5836

Star Creek Farms
Dahlonega, GA 30533
706-216-6770

Sunburst Stables
Route 1
Sautee, GA 30571
706-878-2095

**Trackrock
Riding Academy**
4890 Trackrock
   Campground Road
Blairsville, GA 30512
706-746-5252
Contact: Linda Ford

Twin Oak Stables
Route 1, Box 1264
Blairsville, GA 30512
706-745-5349
Contact: Alton Parker, Jr.

INSTRUCTION/CAMPS

Chastain Park Stables
4371 Powers Ferry Road, N.W.
Atlanta, GA 30327-3416
404-257-1470

Chastain offers lessons to riders of all experience levels from the age of five years. English riding lessons are in seventeen-week semesters. The stable provides only lessons and boarding. There are no rentals or trail rides. (See pages 166–167 for Chastain's therapeutic riding program.)

Reiterhof Equestrian Center
Route 1, Box 1912
Clarkesville, GA 30523
706-754-1284

Reiterhof offers lessons and training for children and adults, from beginners to advanced students. A systematic European foundation is given in dressage and jumping in both indoor and outdoor facilities.

Swan's Nest Farm Monastery
Star Route, Box 246
Marble Hill, GA 30148
706-475-0199

Summer day camp is held for boys and girls, from six to fifteen years old. Camps are limited to fifteen students per week. Training includes one- to six-week programs in horsemanship, handling, care, training, animal communication, and self-awareness. Camps are tailored to basic, intermediate, and advanced experience levels, or they can be customized. Swan's Nest is located in the foothills of the North Georgia mountains, one hour north of the metro Atlanta area.

Winning Ways Equestrian Center
1204 Nebo Road
Dallas, GA 30132
404-443-9018

Day and overnight summer camps for beginners or intermediates ages six to eighteen are offered. Training includes horse safety, proper riding techniques, horse care, showmanship, and equipment maintenance. Instruction is either English or Western saddle. Arena and trail rides are offered, and a horse show is presented.

Sweet Sunshine Equestrian Center
14295 Birmingham Highway
Alpharetta, GA 30201
404-475-8319 or 343-9807

Over 300 acres of trails, three outdoor rings, and a 150-by-300-foot climate-controlled arena are among the amenities at Sweet Sunshine. Lessons, clinics, and summer camps provide combined and dressage training for beginners to advanced riders.

Majesta Stables Summer Camp
4565 Pisgah Road
Cumming, GA 30130
404-887-0209 or 998-9483

At Majesta, the staff trains riders from beginner to advanced experience levels and from ages six and up in English riding. Nine one-week sessions are offered. The stable features an indoor ring. The highlight of the week is the BBQ and camp-out every Thursday.

Sugar Creek Stables
(404) 889-2902
Contact: Bruce Fitzgerald or Janice Gilmore

Sugar Creek boasts a 90-by-250-foot lighted arena and offers lessons and training, or you can bring your own trainer. In addition, the stable offers trail rides and even transportation to and from horse shows.

Broken Arrow Equine Enterprises, Inc.
3350 McGinnis Ferry Road
Alpharetta, GA 30201
404-442-1454 or 343-8387

At Broken Arrow, you can get English and Western lessons indoors or at two outdoor arenas.

Verse Noia Farm
404-623-0657 or 887-6613
Contact: Neil and Linda McClure

Verse Noia has everything from trail rides to fox hunting, as well as lessons and training.

Joan Keegan Combined Training Camp
Flat Creek Stable
Hogansville, GA 30230
706-637-4862 or 637-8920 or 637-8500

Day camp includes training in horse care and management, basic dressage, gridwork and gymnastic jumping, galloping and conditioning, as well as cross country and show jumping.

Big Bear Farm
Pine Mountain, GA 31822
706-663-4583 or 563-2583
Contact: Herb Schneider

Big Bear Farm offers adult combined training.

Horseback riding for the disabled is covered in Chapter 10, "Something for Everyone."

IMPORTANT EVENTS

Check with the following facilities for information on special events: **Chateau Elan Equestrian Show Facility**, 6060 Golf Club Drive, Braselton, GA 30517, 800-847-6705; **Reiterhof Equestrian Center** (see above); **Wills Park Equestrian Center** (see above).

A FINAL NOTE

Under Georgia law, an equine activity sponsor or equine professional is not liable for an injury to or the death of a participant in equine activities resulting from the inherent risks of equine activities, pursuant to Chapter 12 of Title 4 of the official code of Georgia annotated.

6

SAILING

Our idea of the perfect afternoon is a leisurely cruise where we can get a suntan, admire the scenery, and "cottage watch." To other people, however, sailing isn't challenging or exciting unless they're racing. Most clubs sponsor regular or periodic races for their members and occasionally sponsor invitational or open regattas.

If you're an inexperienced sailor, don't be intimidated. One wag suggested that the only thing you need to know about racing is Racing Rule Number One: don't fall off the boat.

There's probably a class of racing for your level of experience. If there's not, sailing against those who are more advanced can be a great learning experience.

While sailing is an occasional pleasure for us, longtime sailors Barney and Peggy Riley are leading an idyllic life doing what they love best: offering sailing lessons and day-, weekend-, or week-long sailboat cruises off the Georgia coast.

Barney is quick to debunk common myths about coastal sailing. You might have heard that the water is too shallow or too muddy, that there is no wind in the summer, that dealing with winds and currents is too complicated. In reality, Barney explains, the water is sixty feet deep and clear once you're offshore.

Barney can wax poetic when extolling the wind conditions. The wind is so reliable and consistent that he describes the 12-knot southeast wind that makes its appearance at 2:00 P.M. every day as a "doctor making house calls." We hate to burst his bubble, but how many doctors do you know who make house calls, especially to the minute?

From their location at the Golden Isles Marina just off St. Simons Island, you can see the Atlantic Ocean. This ideal position allows almost immediate offshore sailing—from Golden Isles you can be out in the ocean in fifteen minutes. After a tranquil or strenuous day of sailing, there's hardly anything more pleasant than a long spinnaker reach through St. Simons Sound while returning to the marina.

While the immensity of the ocean causes many would-be sailors to shy away from cruising there, in actuality it may be more difficult to sail on land-locked lakes, where the wind is often light and prone to shifting direction every few minutes. Regardless of the frustrations and challenges of lake sailing, Georgia's many lakes provide convenient access to the sport. Much sailing on these lakes is individual and/or informal. However, several clubs and organizations offer organized sailing programs and/or sailing lessons.

If sailing appeals to you but you think it's an expensive sport, confined to the upper classes who can afford a boat and its upkeep, there are several avenues open to you. Many coastal and inland marinas maintain rental fleets and offer instruction and/or skippered cruises. Small one-man boats such as Sunfish are relatively inexpensive and completely portable. If you want to race, contact the nearest sailing club; someone is always looking for crew members.

Another sailing alternative is windsurfing, a sport that provides an excellent body workout in addition to the thrill of zipping across the water like a waterbug. The latest addition to the sailing scene is canoe sailing.

COASTAL SAILING

Ocean cruising is an exhilarating experience, evoking the romance of the elegant clipper ships. It's an enchanting way to explore offshore islands and to make trips of several days. However, ocean sailing requires a large boat so that you can sleep and cook aboard. Sailing on the ocean also requires lots of electrical equipment, probably a motor and a dinghy, and a space at a marina, where the boat is always rigged and ready to go. Ocean sailing also demands a thorough knowledge of tides, currents, and channels.

Unfortunately, Georgia's coast is not very conducive to day sailing, by which we mean sailing a boat under twenty-five-feet long, with no sleeping, kitchen, or bathroom facilities. It may require trailering to the site, launching, rigging, and then undoing everything to take it out of the water again.

First of all, there are few public ramps on the coast. From marinas and launches that are situated up coastal rivers—particularly those around Savannah—it can take up to two hours just to make it out to the ocean. It's easy to see that the effort required doesn't leave much time for enjoying the sport.

One way to enjoy ocean sailing is to take lessons or skippered charters from a coastal location. Another is to participate in an invitational or open regatta.

COASTAL SAILING INSTRUCTION

Dunbar Sales, Inc.
115 Marina Drive
Golden Isles Marina
St. Simons, GA 31522
912-638-8573 or 800-282-1411
Contact: Peggy and Barney Riley, Jr.

Barney's theory of teaching is that hands-on experience is more valuable than classroom lessons. "No one would try to learn to play golf without a club in his hands. You can't learn to sail unless you're on a boat," he says. Barney's goal is to teach you sailing with "minimum effort/maximum recreation." He calls his method of teaching "sailing by the numbers." He asks his students to visualize hands on a clock rather than filling their heads with the theories of physics.

Affiliated with the American Sailing Association, Dunbar Sales offers certification courses in basic sailing, coastal cruising, bareboat chartering, coastal navigation, and how to run the Intracoastal waterway. Those courses are recognized all over the United States and in all the major chartering areas of the Caribbean. Both Rileys have Coast Guard captain's licenses and all the Coast Guard Auxiliary certifications available, as well as all levels of instructor certification from the ASA.

The basic sailing school is a four-day program of beginning sailing instruction offered once each month. The coastal cruising school, a weekend program, is also offered once each month. Bareboat certification qualifies you to charter a boat up to forty feet long for overnight trips.

Each class has a maximum of four students who take turns as helmsman, navigator, and spotter, learning through

111

doing. The school is closed from November through mid-March.

Dunbar Sales operates a marine store that offers NOAA charts, DMA charts, chart kits, all government navigation publications, all types of marine equipment, clothing, accessories, and boating supplies. In addition, the company services, sells, and installs marine accessories, roller furling, all types of electronics, freshwater systems, and bilge systems.

If you'd rather leave the sailing to them, you might enjoy one of the Rileys' skippered sailing charters around the barrier islands. In addition to a relaxing cruise, you'll have a supper of mackerel or bass before you get to Cumberland Island if you drag a fishing line behind the boat.

Sail Harbor
618 Wilmington Island Road
Savannah, GA 31410
912-897-2135 or 912-897-2896

Located by the Sheraton Savannah Resort & Country Club, Sail Harbor is one of the largest full-service marinas in the Southeast. Instructional courses include four to five hours of basic sailing, three days of coastal piloting, and an intensive two-day racing clinic. Private instruction is also available. *Sailing World* magazine named the academy "one of the 50 best deals in America." Boats can be chartered with or without a skipper. Choose from full-day, half-day, or sunset skippered charters. A ship's store and the Lightship Tavern & Grill complete the marina.

Sailing School Blackbeard
P.O. Box 19634

Atlanta, GA 30325
404-351-WIND (9463)

Looking as rakish as the pirate after whom the school is named, Joseph Jurskis runs a tight ship—no alcohol, tobacco, or four-letter words are permitted. The former Army Ranger teaches basic and advanced sailing, racing, navigation, and a special course on survival techniques using the total-saturation approach, a four-day (Friday through Monday) marathon of twelve- to sixteen-hour classroom and on-the-water sessions. Participants must pass a written exam with a score of 95 and solo successfully. Jurskis's common-sense coastal navigation theories are offered year-round at three evening sessions in Atlanta. Racing rules and strategies are taught off Darien, Georgia. Advanced students may want to participate in a week-long voyage such as the one from Miami to Abacos, Bahamas.

INLAND SAILING

While inland winds aren't always as reliable as those off the coast, Georgia's many lakes make sailing convenient and accessible for many landlubbers who can't make the long trip to the sea. A Lake Lanier sailor calls inland sailing "connecting the dots—you go from one spot of wind to another." The two most popular sailing lakes are Lanier and Allatoona, on which sailors can find instruction, rentals, racing clubs, and more. One way of breaking into the sport is by crewing. Just call any one of the clubs—they're always looking for crew members.

INSTRUCTION

Lanier Sailing Academy, Ltd.
3271 Fawn Trail
Marietta, GA 30066
404-945-8810

This academy offers both lessons and sailboat rentals. Lessons involve classroom instruction and on-board training. Courses offered include a twenty-four-hour practical sailing class, a twelve-hour basic sailing course, a mini four-hour sailing clinic, a Learn and Cruise course, Women Only sailing classes, coastal navigation and Loran C operation, coastal cruising and bareboat chartering, bareboat check-out certification, bluewater cruising school, weekend racing clinic, junior sailing program, and private instruction. Periodically, a multi-day coastal cruising seminar is offered on location.

The academy's Passport Sailing Club offers unlimited free use of rental boats year-round, social activities, and discounts on boating gear and supplies.

Once you have the basics down pat, you might want to rent a sailboat—particularly if you're thinking about buying one but haven't decided what you want. Lanier Sailing offers a variety of boats from fourteen to thirty feet long. Reservations are required. There is a two-hour minimum, but rentals can be for a half-day, full day, or weekend. Lanier Sailing also offers skippered sunset cruises and charter cruises.

Windsong Sailing Academy
4052 Wrexham Drive
Lithonia, GA 30058
404-256-6700
Contact: Dave Crumbley

Sponsored by community colleges and parks and recreation departments in Cobb, DeKalb, and Gwinnett counties, Windsong offers separate registration for ground theory programs and on-the-water programs. This approach enables intermediate or advanced students to save the time and cost of the theory class. Private and group classes are offered quarterly on a year-round basis.

Classroom courses include basic sailing theory, coastal navigation, celestial navigation I and II, how to buy a boat, annual boat maintenance, and gourmet afloat—tricks and techniques of meal planning, preparation, and spoilage prevention afloat. For on-the-water classes, sailing outings are planned to Lakes Lanier and Allatoona. A three-day course called Basic Coastal Cruising and Bareboat Chartering is conducted in St. Petersburg, Florida. Longer sailing trips where you can practice what you've learned are planned to such exotic destinations as the Dry Tortugas and the British Virgin Islands.

CLUBS

Barefoot Sailing Club
1143 Martin Ridge Road
Roswell, GA 30076
404-256-6839 (twenty-four-hour hotline)

Founded in 1971, the Barefoot Sailing Club is a major yacht racing force on Lake Lanier. The club, which meets monthly, also sponsors numerous clinics, races, and social activities. Learn to Sail courses are held in the spring, while the Novice Race Clinic is held in early summer. The annual two-day Barefoot Open Regatta is run the first weekend of October.

Other activities include the Bikini Sunburn fun day in July, a Campout/Cookout raft-up in August, moonlight cruises, and race cookouts. Races are run almost every weekend with the exception of December through February. Visitors are welcome to race for two days before joining. Membership includes the newsletter "Footnotes."

Lake Lanier Sailing Club
6206 Commodore Drive
Flowery Branch, GA 30542
404-967-6441

LLSC is the envy of Lake Lanier. In the first place, it has property and a clubhouse that sits on the tip of a shady peninsula, with a sweeping panorama of the lake. Not that you'll find members lolling about enjoying the view—they're out racing. With several fleets including Lasers, J22s and J24s, Lightnings, Thistles, and Butterflies, races are conducted every weekend—including a Frostbite Series in the winter. The club also sponsors several open races and regattas each year and even holds a windsurfing event in the summer.

The club offers extensive docking facilities to members as well as a launch ramp and on-land storage areas—both covered and uncovered. New members are welcome, be they old salts or novices. LLSC also has a liberal reciprocity policy for visiting sailors from clubs in other parts of the country or world and acts as the semipermanent host for the Georgia Tech Sailing Club. LLSC runs a junior program for ten- to seventeen-year-olds and also sponsors some ladies' racing clinics.

Southern Sailing Club
2141 Fairway Circle N.E.

Atlanta, GA 30319
404-296-5600

The club, which sails on Lake Lanier, sponsors several race series as well as numerous social events throughout the year. The club maintains a hotline and publishes a newsletter called "The Masthead."

Other sailing organizations include the Atlanta Inland Sailing Club, Southern Atlanta Yacht Racing Association, Dixie Inland Yacht Racing Association, and the Atlanta Yacht Club, which is based at Lake Allatoona.

WINDSURFING

If you've been thinking about trying windsurfing but haven't made a resolution to do so, consider the experience of one young couple we know. They met windsurfing on a blustery winter day at Lake Lanier. He's from England, working in Georgia temporarily. They probably would never have met if it weren't for their shared interest in windsurfing. Enthusiasm for the sport led to marriage. Now they're sailing off into the sunset together.

We can't guarantee such happy endings, but consider some of the other advantages of windsurfing. The sport provides a dynamic workout. Although it appears that windsurfers use the upper body exclusively, they actually use the lower body as well. The exercise is extremely beneficial for the back. You may find the learning process frustrating, but don't underestimate the physical benefit you get from falling off, getting back on, and hauling the sail out of the water. Windsurfing is a sport that you can enjoy alone or in groups, and you can sail on almost any body of water. A sailboard is considerably more economical than a sailboat, and you can carry it on your car.

Georgia has so many lakes and such a mild climate that windsurfing is popular for most of the year. It is also widely pursued off the coast, where the wind is stronger and more reliable. Most Atlantans who partake in the sport do so at Lake Lanier. The only problem is that the wind is much better in the winter, when you really don't want to get wet and chilled. A wetsuit can solve that problem.

BOARD SAILING

Atlanta Board Sailing Club
P.O. Box 28376
Atlanta, GA 30358
404-634-0537

If you're interested in windsurfing, you might want to join the Atlanta Board Sailing Club. It provides instruction, racing, and social activities for windsurfing enthusiasts. The club meets monthly for an educational program on such topics as equipment, sailing technique, racing skills, and vacation destinations, followed by a social hour.

The club sponsors five regattas at Lake Lanier each year. People who haven't tried sailboard racing are encouraged to come and participate in the B Fleet (Novice Division). At some races, a Workshop Fleet is held for first-time racers. Mini-clinics are held before the races to cover rules, the course to be sailed, and starting procedures. All you need is a full-size board (between 11 and 12.5 feet long). Short-board sailors enjoy the Slalom Series, informal racing during the windy season. The club also sponsors a Learn to Windsurf Day in

July. Some members are such avid racers that they travel to regattas throughout the Southeast. The club also lobbies for windsurfing in the areas of safety and water access.

Membership includes participation in all meetings and activities, racing discounts, a monthly newsletter, and information concerning new and used equipment.

CANOE SAILING

If you're just looking for something new and unusual, want a versatile vessel, or don't want to invest a lot of money in a sailboat, you might consider canoe sailing. Some manufacturers of larger canoes—those sixteen feet and longer—also produce masts, booms, and sails to fit the vessels. You'll need a broad-based canoe for stability.

7
FLAT-WATER
PADDLING SPORTS

*If people concentrated on the really important things in life,
there'd be a shortage of paddles.*
—Georgia Canoeing Association

Paddling sports, canoeing and kayaking, permit a paddler to explore lakes, rivers, and coastal areas alone as well as in groups. Paddling also affords optimum pleasure for enthusiasts who paddle for the pure joy of it, without a destination in mind.

The sport provides one of the best upper-body and cardiovascular low-impact workouts you can get. When done correctly, paddling works all the large muscles of the torso, because it involves a twisting motion, rather than a pulling motion as in rowing. The upper body and abdomen include some of the largest muscle groups in the body, and when you use them, rather than only your arm muscles, you are working more efficiently and tire less easily.

In canoeing, you'll exercise your leg muscles if you use them to provide more power. In kayaking, especially sea kayaking, the legs are used even more because they control the rudder.

QUIET PADDLING

Georgia's numerous state parks and power-generation lakes provide infinite possibilities for paddling. Once south of the fall line, most of the state's rivers provide quiet-water paddling. Coastal marshes are best explored by canoe or kayak.

Some of the best places to paddle in Georgia are the Augusta Canal, Altamaha River, Turkey Creek, Stevens Creek, Savannah River, Ogeechee River, Flint River, Toccoa River, Sweetwater Creek State Conservation Park, and the Okefenokee Swamp.

Augusta Canal

Augusta Canal Authority
801 Broad Street, Room 507
Augusta, GA 30901
706-722-1071

The nine-mile Augusta Canal parallels the Savannah River. It is not only a National Historic Landmark, but is claimed to be the best example in the country of an efficient and fully industrial/recreational canal system. From the very beginning in 1846, the canal was a major route for transporting people, materials, and cotton as well as being enjoyed by the citizens as a recreational waterway for picnics and other leisure outings. The canal is being restored and refurbished so that it and the landmark buildings will be preserved.

You can put your canoes in at several locations from below the dam at Bull Sluice to 13th Street, allowing canoeing on almost the entire nine-mile length of the canal. You can also canoe on Lakes Warren and Olmstead, which have inlets into the canal. There is a canoe portage between the Savannah River and the canal at the Clearing. The distance from the dam to Interstate 20 is 2.05 miles; from the dam to the pumping station 3.5 miles; from the dam to 13th Street 7.0 miles; and from the dam to Riverwalk 8.5 miles.

The current can be deceptively violent and subject to sudden increases caused by releases from dams upstream. Always wear a life jacket when boating on the river or the canal. Gas-powered motor craft are not permitted in the canal, nor is swimming allowed.

If you want to rent a canoe on the Augusta Canal, **American Wilderness Outfitters, Ltd.,** is conveniently located near the canal. American Wilderness rents professional outdoor equipment for half days and full days. Canoe rentals include two life jackets, two paddles, and a foam block kit for those who want to transport the canoe themselves. Shuttle service is provided for an additional fee. The company also rents tents and the new "sit-on-top" touring kayaks. Contact hours are Monday through Friday 4:00 P.M. to 6:00 P.M., all day Saturday, and Sunday by appointment.

American Wilderness Outfitters, Ltd.
Augusta Business Center
Augusta, GA 30907
706-860-0278 or beeper 737-1661
Contact: Jim Stringer

Little St. Simons Island
P.O. Box 1078

St. Simons, GA 31522
912-638-7472
Contact: Deborah McIntyre

Providing relief from the everyday world, the privately owned barrier island of Little St. Simons lies adjacent to heavily developed St. Simons and is accessible only by a twice-daily private ferry. The Berolzheimer family uses the island much of the year, but during certain periods it is open to overnight guests. The 10,000-acre island caters to a maximum of only twenty-four guests at a time with a staff of seventeen, including two full-time naturalists and an intern, a stable manager, fishing and boating guides, and an outstanding kitchen staff.

The resort has several canoes, kayaks, and flat-bottomed fishing boats with trolling motors that are ideal for exploring the maze of hidden waterways in and around the island. The guides will either take you out to their favorite spot if they aren't busy, or direct you to them. If you're not back by the expected time, someone will come looking for you.

Flint River

Canoe the Flint
4429 Woodland Road
State 36 at Flint River
Thomaston, GA 30286
404-647-2633
Contact: Jim and Margie McDaniel

The company offers guided and self-guided trips on the Flint River as well as rental canoes and rafts, a shuttle upriver, and canoe and kayak lessons. It is open on weekends April through October, daily from Memorial Day through Labor Day, and other times by reservation.

Altamaha River

A fifteen-mile section west of Darien on the Georgia coast provides good canoeing as well as soothing scenery and glimpses of wildlife as you pass through the Lewis Island Natural Area and the Altamaha State Waterfowl Management Area.

WILDERNESS CANOEING

Okefenokee National Wildlife Refuge

U.S. Fish and Wildlife Service
Okefenokee National Wildlife Refuge
Route 2, Box 338
Folkston, GA 31537
912-496-3331

This 400,000-square-mile park offers 107 miles of canoe trails on fifteen trails that wind through cypress forests and open "prairies." Trail trips range from two days (fourteen miles) to five days (forty-three miles). Each canoe trail is limited to one party per day, and each party is limited to a maximum of ten canoes and/or twenty people. The minimum party size is two people.

Canoe trails into the Okefenokee Wilderness can be reserved in advance by telephone only. Reservations can be made no earlier than two months to the day in advance of the intended departure date. Call 912-496-3331, Monday through

Friday, 7:00 A.M. until 3:30 P.M. During the seasonal peak from March through April, individuals, groups, and organizations are limited to one trip.

You can reverse the starting point and destination, but only by permit. Boat launching and entrance fees are required at Stephen Foster State Park and the Suwannee Canal Recreation Area. Make sure you are in good enough physical condition to make the full trip, because motors are not permitted on canoe trips. Swamp terrain is flat and there is no fast water and very little dry land, so you will have to paddle constantly. You may have to get out and push across peat blowups or shallow water. In addition, short portages may be necessary. If the water becomes too low to permit use of certain trails, as occasionally it does, you will be notified.

From June through September, the weather is hot and humid, with daytime temperatures above 90° F. Winter days can fluctuate between 40° and 80° during the day but averages in the 50s and 60s. Summer nights are warm, and winter nights can be at or near freezing. The rainy season is generally June through September.

Each traveler is required by law to have a Coast Guard–approved life preserver in his possession. Each canoe must contain a compass and a flashlight. Canoeists must register when entering and leaving the swamp. Due to danger from alligators, pets are not permitted in boats, swimming is prohibited, and you may not trail fish you've caught on a stringer. You must launch by 10:00 A.M. to ensure that you can reach your overnight stop before dark.

Overnight camping is permitted only at designated overnight stops, which are usually raised, covered platforms. You must remain at the site from sunset to sunrise.

Suggested supplies include a rope for pulling the canoe, drinking water, insect repellent, mosquito netting, rain gear,

125

a first-aid kit, extra batteries, litter bags, a pop-up tent and/or jungle hammock, and a sleeping bag.

Canoes, camping equipment, and services are available for rent from the concessionaire at the Suwannee Canal Recreation Area at the Folkston entrance to the swamp or at the Stephen C. Foster State Park entrance at Fargo.

Suwannee Canal Recreation Concession, Inc.
Route 2, Box 336
Folkston, GA 31537
912-496-7156

Stephen C. Foster
State Park
Route 1, Box 131
Fargo, GA 31631
912-637-5274

Wilderness Southeast
711 Sandtown Road
Savannah, GA 31410
912-897-5108

CANOEING AROUND ATLANTA

Providence Outdoor Recreation Center/
Fulton County Parks
13313 Providence Road
Alpharetta, GA 30201
404-740-2419

Located in a northern suburb of Atlanta, the park offers canoeing lessons as well as canoeing on the Chattahoochee. Day trips are scheduled at least one Saturday each month. Other weekend and/or weekday trips can be arranged. Canoes and canoe transport are available.

Chattahoochee River Park/
Fulton County Parks and Recreation

203 Azalea Drive
Roswell, GA 30075
404-640-3055

Canoe/kayak owners can also put in their craft at the Chattahoochee River Park, from which you can paddle about a mile
upstream to the Georgia 400 bridge and downstream about
four miles to Morgan Falls Dam.

KAYAKING

Once upon a time, the word "kayak" conjured up a vision of a
fur-clad Eskimo slicing through what little open water there
was between icebergs or glaciers. Lately, we've been more
likely to envision nerves-of-steel white-water river runners
crashing over rapids. In fact, however, kayaking can offer a
relaxing flat-water experience as well.

The stability and comfort of touring kayaks make them a
perfect method for a family outing for both novices and experienced paddlers—everyone from youngsters to seniors. In
addition to rivers and streams, coastal islands, marsh creeks,
and secluded beaches are easily accessible by stable touring
kayaks.

Several outfitters provide not only equipment, but guided
trips.

Devil's Race Course

Located on the Chattahoochee River at Powers Ferry, this

127

kayak race course is maintained by the Atlanta Whitewater Club. Open to the general public, the course consists of a series of movable gates suspended over the water to create a slalom course where kayakers can practice various turns and techniques at every experience level, from beginner to expert. Several Olympic hopefuls live in nearby apartments so they can have easy access to the course.

Sea Kayaking

We've included sea kayaking in Chapter 9 because you must know how to handle waves, tides, and currents. However, once you've crested the breakers, kayaking at sea is very similar to kayaking on flat water.

KAYAKING OUTFITTERS

Kayaking Adventures/Shooo Cow Kayak Company
P.O. Box 82
Tallulah Falls, GA 30573
706-754-5885
Contact: Ray Santa or Bonnie Haggerty

Ray and Bonnie offer a guided tour of lakes and rivers around Tallulah Falls in Northeast Georgia. The trip includes a touring kayak, paddle, Personal Flotation Device (PFD), sprayskirt, dry bag for personal items, and gourmet lunch or snack depending on the length of the trip. Modern kayaks feature watertight hatches for picnic baskets, coolers, fishing rods, and other items. Half-day and full-day trips are offered, and reservations are required.

KAYAK NATURE TOURS

Ocean Motion
1300 Ocean Boulevard
St. Simons, GA 31522
912-638-5225

Ocean Motion offers guided two-hour tours of the coastal islands. The package includes equipment and an introductory instructional clinic.

CANOE POLING AND SAILING

Some folks are always looking for new challenges. The newest quiet-water sports we've heard of are canoe poling and canoe sailing. Canoe poling is just what it sounds like: you stand up in the canoe and propel it with a long pole. We envision an immaculately dressed Victorian gentleman punting along an English river with his lady fair. However, punts are flat-bottomed and very stable. Canoe poling requires flat, shallow water, a broad-based canoe, and an excellent sense of balance. The waters of the Okefenokee Swamp would be just the thing if it weren't for the fact that you could be attacked by an alligator if you should happen to tip over.

Canoe sailing also requires a broad-based canoe. Manufacturers of larger canoes—those sixteen feet and larger—produce sail packages including a mast, boom, and sail.

RAFTING/TUBING

Some folks would rather float than paddle, or paddle only sporadically. Floating down a lazy river in a rubber raft is popular in the North Georgia mountains and in metro Atlanta. A favorite summer pastime is to load up your raft with lunch and beverages and float for hours. If you get too hot, just splash yourself or pull up to shore and take a quick dip.

Chattahoochee Outdoor Center
1990 Island Ford Parkway
Dunwoody, GA 30350
404-395-6851

Points of rental are Johnson Ferry Road at the river and Interstate North Parkway at the river, May through Labor Day. Rentals include paddles and life jackets. Coolers and other equipment and supplies can be rented additionally, or you can bring your own. Shuttle service is available from all locations at an additional cost. Glass containers are not permitted on the river between Morgan Falls Dam and Paces Mill.

Float times and distances are as follows:

• Morgan Falls Dam to Johnson Ferry—two miles; one-half to one hour in a canoe, one to two hours in a raft.

• Johnson Ferry to Powers Island—3.5 miles; one to three hours in a canoe, two to four hours in a raft.

• Powers Island to Paces Mill—three miles; one to two hours in a canoe, one to three hours in a raft.

OTHER OUTFITTERS IN THE METRO ATLANTA AREA

Atlanta Rent-A-Raft, Inc.
2779 Delk Road, S.E.
Marietta, GA 30067
404-952-2824

Chattahoochee Canoe & Raft Rental
199 Azalea Drive
Roswell, GA 30075
404-996-7778

Georgia Outdoors
6518 Roswell Road, N.W.
Atlanta, GA 30328
404-256-4048

Pro Leisure, Inc.
679 Johnson Ferry Road, N.E.
Marietta, GA 30068
404-971-5555

The Northeast Georgia mountains offer a plethora of canoeing, kayaking, rafting, and tubing adventures.

Alpine Tubing
Route 1, Box 1485
Helen, GA 30545
706-878-TUBE
Contact: Shirley Musacchio

Broad River Outpost
Route 3, Box 3449
Danielsville, GA 30633
706-795-3242
Contact: Bud Freeman

**Amicalola River Rafting
Outpost**
P.O. Box 683
Dawsonville, GA 30534
706-265-6892
Contact: Bill Dulaney

Garden Tubing Ltd.
Helen, GA 30545
706-878-1359

Wildwood Shop
P.O. Box 119, River Street
Helen, GA 30545
706-865-4451

Appalachian Outfitters
P.O. Box 793
Dahlonega, GA 30533
706-864-7117
Contact: Ben or Dana
    LaChance

Cool River Tubing
706-878-COOL

Covering 3.5 miles and taking 2.5 hours, this tube ride is
the longest and coolest tube ride in Helen, according to the

131

company. Rides are offered seven days a week in season. Located on Edelweiss Drive on the river behind the Outlet Mall, Cool River provides free parking, shuttles, and picnic tables.

MISCELLANEOUS

Georgia Canoeing Association
P.O. Box 7023
Atlanta, GA 30357
404-421-9729

Contact the club for general information about paddling sports—canoeing, kayaking, and rafting—on both flat- and white-water rivers as well as oceans and estuaries. Founded in 1966, GCA offers training in general canoeing, safety, racing, exploration, and recreation. The club, which stresses conservation, is active year-round with monthly meetings, scheduled trips, and social functions such as a camping/paddling/partying weekend each fall and spring.

These outfitters offer good advice as well as equipment:

Call of the Wild
425 Market Place
Roswell, GA 30075
404-992-5400

Go With the Flow
4 Elizabeth Way
Roswell, GA 30075
404-992-3208

For information on water levels, call the TVA Water Resources Line, 800-238-2264.

Bibliography

Estes, Carter and Almquist. *Canoe Trails of the Deep South.* Birmingham, AL: Menasha Ridge Press, 1993.

Sehlinger, Bob. *Paddler's Guide to North Georgia.* Birmingham, AL: Menasha Ridge Press, 1993.

SHOOTING SPORTS

Firing at clay projectiles is the perfect solution for the sportsman who likes the challenge of shooting but opposes using live targets, or for the hunter who wants to hone his skills. You can participate in the sport no matter what your age or income. Many physically challenged people are able to join in as well. Families often take part in the sport together, and there are a growing number of women champions. Current variations of shooting sports include American and international trap, American and international skeet, sporting clays, and five-stand sporting clays.

TRAP

Trapshooting began in eighteenth-century England, where English noblemen would shoot live pigeons released from a trap. Over the years, other targets, such as "metal" birds with rotary wings and feather-filled glass balls, were developed to replace live birds. The game was introduced to the United States in 1831.

Trap is the most popular clay target shooting sport in America, with 55,000 active shooters who fire at an estimated 82.5 million registered targets a year.

A round of modern trap singles, also called the sixteen-yard event, consists of shooting twenty-five clay targets thrown from a low "traphouse" located sixteen yards in front of the firing line. The targets fly at various angles that the shooter cannot predict and are usually broken at an average range of thirty-five yards. In a regulation round, five targets are shot from each of five stations.

Five shooters are involved. Beginning with Station 1, each shooter fires one shot in turn until all have fired five times. Then everyone moves to the next station, continuing in this manner until the round is completed. Sixteen-yard trap is best for a beginner. More experienced trap-shooters enjoy "handicap trap," which involves standing longer distances, up to twenty-seven yards, behind the traphouse. In another variation, "doubles trap," two targets are thrown simultaneously.

International trap is often called bunker, trench, Olympic trap, or international clay pigeon. In the international version, targets are thrown farther, at varying degrees of elevation, and at a more extreme angle. The targets are composed of more rigid material.

International trap uses fifteen machines located in an underground bunker 16.5 yards in front of five shooting stations. There are three traps in front of each station, each set to throw targets at various angles and elevations. International targets are thrown 50 percent farther. Squads consist of six shooters.

SKEET

Skeet was developed in 1920 by a group of Massachusetts sportsmen seeking to improve their shooting skills. The original layout of the skeet field was a complete circle with a shooting station at each number on a clock face. A single trap at the twelve o'clock position threw targets over the six o'clock position. This version of the game was called "shooting around the clock." As the sport developed, the circle was cut in half.

The field has eight stations from which the gunner breaks targets thrown from two traphouses—a "high house" located behind Station 1 and a "low house" behind Station 7. During a round of American skeet, a shooter will fire at twenty-five targets consisting of singles thrown one at a time from the high or low house and double targets thrown, one from each house, simultaneously. A high and low house single is shot from each station, and doubles are fired from Stations 1, 2, 6, and 7, totaling twenty-four shots. The twenty-fifth target is called the "option" and is a repeat of the first miss. Skeet is shot in squads of five shooters or fewer. In tournaments, doubles events require a minimum of fifty targets.

In skeet the shooter has more control than in trap because he points his gun in a specified direction and calls "pull" when he is ready. Skeet is considered a more social sport than trap.

International skeet, also known as Olympic skeet, is somewhat different from American skeet. The course eliminates the optional shot and the relatively easy singles from stations 1 and 7. Targets fly from farther away. Each machine has a built-in electronic delay switch that randomly selects and delays launching for zero to three seconds. A round of registered targets consists of 200 to 400 targets shot in series of twenty-five. There is always a shoot-off at International skeet tournaments.

SPORTING CLAYS

Sporting clays originated in the 1920s in Great Britain. Unlike other clay shooting games that are built to rigid dimensions, sporting clays courses are designed to blend in with the environment. Most sporting clays fields are laid out over ten to fifty acres consisting of several environments, such as fields and woods, each simulating the habitat of a different game bird. Each field contains one or more stations to provide a variety of shots from a minimum number of machines—for example, singles, doubles, following pairs, and rabbits. Mobile stations permit changes in the course for additional challenge.

Sporting clays has expanded worldwide and is recognized as a tournament sport and a major recreational clay target shooting sport. America's fastest-growing shooting sport, sporting clays is particularly popular with families. Many resorts have added sporting clays to their recreational activities, and business travelers often abandon golf for sporting clays. In fact, sporting clays has been compared to "golf with a shotgun." Charity tournaments sponsored by conservation organizations such as Ducks Unlimited and Quail Unlimited draw large numbers of shooters.

One of the sport's appeals is unpredictability. Trap and

skeet, while challenging, offer predictable shots repetitively. Sporting clays is the closest thing to real hunting. Targets thrown simulate the sudden appearance of birds or rabbits.

FIVE-STAND SPORTING CLAYS

This new game from the National Sporting Clays Association has several different skill levels from which to choose. It offers shooters the challenge of target combinations using six or eight automatic traps simulating game birds, including teal, dove, quail, and pheasant, as well as bolting rabbits and specialty targets such as battue and midi. Targets can be released in a predetermined sequence or in a sequence unknown to the shooter.

Events consist of twenty-five, fifty, seventy-five, or 100 targets shot from five stands, five shots from each stand, with shooters rotating from stand to stand. The portable stands fit easily onto any existing skeet or trap field. Endless numbers of target flights and combinations can be created by varying the field layout, changing the trap location and/or elevation, target or direction.

GENERAL SAFETY TIPS FOR TRAP, SKEET, AND SPORTING CLAYS

• Always keep the action of your gun open until you are on the firing line and it is your turn to shoot.
• Do not load more than one shell in the gun for trap, two for skeet.
• Keep your gun pointed in a safe direction at all times.

OUTSTANDING CLUBS AND RESORTS

To shoot at some clubs, you must be a member.

Wolf Creek Skeet and Trap Club
3070 Merk Rd.
Atlanta, GA 30349
404-346-8382
Contact: Dan Mitchell

Wolf Creek is not only an outstanding facility, but it is unusual in that it is a Fulton County Park. Already enlarged to nineteen combination skeet and trap fields, ten of which are lighted, Wolf Creek has been chosen to host the 1996 Summer Olympics shooting events. Nineteen million dollars in improvements will be pumped into the park for the Olympics.

Located in the southern Atlanta metro area, the range is only minutes from Atlanta Hartsfield International Airport. The present facilities include a lodge-style clubhouse that contains a cozy great room with comfortable sofas grouped around the stone fireplace, a complete kitchen, a small dining area called the Bullet Hole, and a fully stocked Pro Shop. The paved parking area is equipped with full electric and sanitary hookups for campers.

Managed by Dan Mitchell, a champion all-American skeet shooter and former captain of the U.S. Navy Skeet Team, the club sponsors league shooting, Learn-to-Shoot classes, and registered tournaments. The Wednesday Night League shoots a different clay sport each time. The facility has hosted such events as the National Skeet Shooting Junior World Championships, the U.S. Open, the U.S. Armed Forces Championships, the Ducks Unlimited Continental Shoot, and the Pepsi Pro-Am. In fact, Wolf Creek has an event almost every weekend.

Forest City Gun Club
9203 Ferguson Avenue
Savannah, GA 31406
912-354-0210
Contact: John Culpepper, Manager

The World Skeet Championships are held at this impressive club near Savannah. The imposing facility boasts a large club-house with a bar, double fireplaces enhanced with bird and duck tiles, comfortable leather sofa and chairs grouped around the fireplace, a dining area, a separate dining room, a separate group room, rocking chairs on the covered patio, and even a playground.

Sea Island Gun Club
The Cloister
Box 296
Sea Island, GA 31561
912-638-3611 or 638-8958
Contact: Dick Gardner

The Sea Island Gun Club is an amenity of the prestigious Cloister resort. You can get private instruction from World Champion Fred Missildine by appointment. Call 912-638-2067. In addition to buying shells and targets, you can rent a gun.

This facility has a gorgeous panorama of the shooting range as well as the palmettos waving over the Marshes of Glynn. The cozy semicircular clubhouse sports a fireplace and is furnished with sofas and chairs. Rattan chairs are lined up along the windows so spectators can enjoy the view. Hours vary according to the season, so be sure to call ahead.

Callaway Gardens Gun Club
P.O. Box 2000
Pine Mountain, GA 31822-2000
706-663-5129
Contact: Ernie Wilkins

Although this is a membership club, it is open to Callaway guests and to the public. The club, which offers both trap and skeet, is credited with introducing sporting clays to Georgia.

The club is operated under the direction of modest Ernie Wilkins, who wouldn't tell us all the titles he's won. What we do know is that he has competed and won in state and world championships for over thirty years, and taught and coached for over twenty-five years, including coaching several world champions and serving on the board of directors for the Georgia State Shooting Association. "I've derived far more pleasure from seeing students I've taught win than I ever did from winning myself," he says. Ernie certainly showed us the ropes.

The sporting clays course wanders through fields and lightly wooded areas, simulating a real hunting experience. An intimate clubhouse features a members' lounge. Several important annual events include a benefit for the American Cancer Society on the first Saturday in March and two major tournaments—the Magnolia on the first weekend in June and the Prunifolia on the last weekend in July.

Cherokee Rose Shooting Resort
895 Baptist Camp Road

P.O. Drawer 509
Griffin, GA 30224
404-228-2529 or 800-421-2529

Cherokee Rose was named "Best shooting facility in America" by *Gun Digest Book of Sporting Clays* in 1992. Steve Middleditch, 1990 World Professional Clay Target Champion from Dorset County, England, heads the resort's school, which offers trap, skeet, sporting clays, five-stand sporting clays, arena games, and an outdoor rifle and pistol range. Many of these areas are covered and/or lighted for night use. In addition, the resort features a full-service restaurant, a retail store called the StraightShooter, and accommodations for up to six at the rustic Hunting Lodge. Shooting club memberships entitle members to up to 40 percent savings, member-only and member-guest tournaments, and fun shoots, as well as a newsletter.

Specifically, the resort features:

• Championship sporting clays on fully automated and lighted championship courses using twenty-five, fifty, or 100 target rounds

• Five-stand sporting clays with fully automated, multiple target angles and speeds from several shooting stands

• Dove towers where multiple "wobble" traps launch targets from sixty-foot towers for exciting pass shooting

• Duck Shoot where three automatic traps launch targets over water

• Super sporting clays that boast a multistand course for smaller gauges (.410 and 28), unique in the South

• Starshot course, one of only four in the country, is a night event where the target is released from one of four traps and the score varies by what "zone" the target is broken in

• Gattlinguns where shooters can "flush" up to eight traps on an automated Fantastic Arena

• A pistol and rifle range where shooters fire from a fifty-yard range using a variety of targets, .22 caliber rimfire to .357 magnum centerfire and pistol

Myrtlewood Plantation
P.O. Box 32
Thomasville, GA 31799
912-228-6232
Contact: Bob Carson

Myrtlewood offers sporting clays on a fifteen-field, twenty-four-station course spread out over fifty beautifully landscaped acres. The plantation also offers instruction, a club house, and lodge rentals.

OTHER CLUBS/FACILITIES

Some of the following facilities require memberships.

Athens Rifle Club
1131 Hollow Creek Lane
Watkinsville, GA 30677
706-549-0936
Contact: Henry Burke

Cat Creek Sporting Clays
P.O. Box 52
Pavo, GA 31778
912-686-7700
Contact: Buddy Lewis

Burge Plantation
Route 1, Morehouse Road
Mansfield, GA 30255
706-787-5152
Contact: Paul Stevenson

Cherokee Gun Club
3323 Indian Trail
Gainesville, GA 30506
404-531-9493
Contact: Jack Crowder

Chickasaw Rod & Gun Club
P.O. Box 191
Pelham, GA 31779
912-294-8240
Contact: R.G. Rogers, Sr.

Elbert County Gun Club
Route 2, Box 644
Carlton, GA 30627
404-797-3609
Contact: Mike Mitternick

Flint Skeet & Trap Club
P.O. Box 70058
Albany, GA 31707
912-432-6603
Contact: Jack M. Jones

Griffin Gun Club, Inc.
P.O. Box 100
Barnesville, GA 30204
404-228-4872
Contact: Ben Moore

Little River Gun Club
205 Avenue B
Carrollton, GA 30117
404-832-9553
Contact: Clifford Jiles, Sr.

Meadows National Gun Club
P.O. Box 377
Smarr, GA 31086
912-994-9910
Contact: Cliff Evans or
  Hugh Sosebee, Jr.

Millpond Championship Sporting Clays
Route 1
DeSoto, GA 31743
912-874-6721
Contact: Oscar Tye

Millrock Clay Bird Club, Inc.
2855 Old Atlanta Road
Cumming, GA 30130
404-889-3024
Contact: Albert Leverett

Ocmulgee River Gun Club
169 Marcar Road
Macon, GA 31206
912-788-7989
Contact: Ed Bowden

**Okefenokee
Sporting Clays**
Route 2, Box 435
Folkston, GA 31537
912-496-2417
Contact: H. J. "Ronnie"
 Murray, Sr.

**Pickens County
Sportsman's Club, Inc.**
P.O. Box 824
Jasper, GA 30143
706-635-5095
Contact: A. Bradley Rutledge

**Pigeon Mountain
Sporting Clays**
1643 Camp Road
Chickamauga, GA 30707
706-539-2287
Contact: Mel or Teda Huskey

**Pinetucky Skeet &
Trap Club**
2676 Gordon Highway
Augusta, GA 30909
706-592-4230
Contact: Dan Mumpower

**Robins Skeet &
Trap Range**
2669 US 27
Kathleen, GA 31047
912-926-4500
Contact: Alan Ray

**Shirahland Plantation
and Sporting Clays**
Route 1, Box 340
Camilla, GA 31730
912-734-4522
Contact: Ray Shirah

South River Gun Club
157 North Salem Road
Conyers, GA 30207
404-786-9456
Contact: Jim Clark

Tri-County Gun Club
P.O. Box 1815
Odum, GA 31555
912-586-2723
Contact: Ray Russell

INSTRUCTION

Most of the places listed above offer instruction. In addition, contact expert Jerry Meyer, author of *The Clay Target Handbook* (Lyons & Burford, Publishers, 1992) and *The Sporting Clays Handbook* (Lyons & Burford, Publishers, 1990). Meyer, a full-time instructor and writer, is chairman of the National Sporting Clays Association Instructor Certification Committee as well as a member of the NSCA Advisory Council. Contact:

Jerry Meyer
Route 1, Box 309
Talking Rock, GA 30175
706-276-3363

ORGANIZATIONS

Georgia Skeet Shooting Association
Dave Johnson
2192 Rodeo Drive
Lilburn, GA 30247
404-979-6364 (h)

Quail Unlimited
P.O. Box 10041
Augusta, GA 30903

SPECIAL EVENTS

In addition to the World Championships at Forest City and the two events at Callaway Gardens, just a few of the other events include:

**Peach State Classic
Final Shootout**
The Meadows National
　Gun Club
Smarr, GA 31086
912-994-9910
(November)

Shirahland Fall Blast
Shirahland Plantation
Newton, GA
(December)

**Annual Hays Lewis
Christmas Charity**
Cherokee Rose Shooting
　Resort
Griffin, GA 30224
404-228-2529 or 800-
　421-2529
(December)

Classification Shoots
Cherokee Rose Shooting
　Resort
Griffin, GA
(November)

**Ducks Unlimited
Continental Shoot**
Wolf Creek Trap and
　Skeet Club
3070 Merk Road
Atlanta, GA 30349
404-346-8382
(April)

9
WHITE-WATER CANOEING, KAYAKING, AND RAFTING

Since we don't like carnival rides any more adventurous than the merry-go-round, this is one sport we decided we didn't need to experience firsthand—even for the sake of the book. We're more than happy to take others' word for it.

The official motto of the Georgia Canoeing Association is "River running is a wet, tough job but someone has to do it." Enthusiasts claim that "Georgia is to kayaking as Colorado is to skiing." In fact, the state boasts three of the top ten white-water rivers in the country—Chattooga, Ocoee, and Nantahala (most of the Ocoee and Nantahala are actually in North Carolina). What was once the land of the Cherokee Indians, in the North Georgia mountains, still displays spectacular natural waterfalls, thundering rapids, calm scenic lakes, and mountain flora and fauna. Much of the wilderness area can be explored only via water.

Made famous by the movie *Deliverance* in 1972, the Chattooga River was declared a National Wild and Scenic River

148

in 1974, thus preserving this wilderness river in its primitive state. The Chattooga is a free-flowing river with water levels varying from turbulent high water in the spring to the relaxed lower levels of fall. Carving its way down a steep gorge as it tumbles through the Chattahoochee and Sumter National Forests between Georgia and South Carolina, the Chattooga offers easy to moderate rapids in Section III and tight, technical drops in Section IV.

The four sections offer different degrees of difficulty and permit only certain activities, as follows:

     I.   Moderate—fishing, no boats
    II.   Moderate—canoes and kayaks
   III.   Twelve miles of class III and IV rapids
   IV.   Class V and VI rapids

Selected to host the 1996 Olympic white-water events, the Ocoee River is one of the most popular white-water runs in the country—five miles of action-packed continuous Class III and IV white water. Site of the oldest flume-type hydroelectric project in the United States, the Ocoee's flow is dam controlled.

The Chattahoochee, Etowah, and Chestatee Rivers also have some white water.

ENJOYING THE WHITE-WATER EXPERIENCE

Most white-water trips require significant physical exertion. On many rafting expeditions, for example, everyone has to help carry the rafts in and out of the protected river corridor. In addition, some journeys end with a long paddle across a lake. White-water sports entail risks, including injury and loss of life. You should be in good physical condition and not significantly overweight before you undertake a white-water experience.

Plan to get wet. No matter what the weather, you'll get splashed, and most trips operate rain or shine. In the summer, you'll need shorts or a bathing suit, T-shirt, tennis or river shoes, a towel, and a change of clothes. In cool weather, you'll need wool socks, gloves, a sweater, and a cap. You might even want to wear Thermax or Polypro underwear. Many outfitters provide a wet suit or protective nylon outerwear at no charge, but some do not, so ask. In any season, it's advisable to bring sunglasses, sunscreen, and a hat or visor.

OUTFITTERS

Appalachian Outfitters
P.O. Box 793
Dahlonega, GA 30533
706-864-7117

Appalachian Outfitters offers canoe trips on the Chestatee and Etowah Rivers. These junkets are appropriate for beginners and intermediates. The company also offers rentals, clinics, and professional guides.

Clinics taught by experienced American Canoe Association certified instructors are scheduled the third weekends of April, May, and June to teach basic and white-water canoeing skills, as well as river dynamics and safety. Class I river skills are taught on Saturdays, while Sundays are spent learning how to safely paddle Class II to III white water. Solo and tandem instruction is available. All necessary equipment, transportation, and lunches are provided, as well as recommendations on local lodging or camping facilities.

Appalachian rents canoes and all necessary accessories—life jackets, paddles, floating containers, and knee pads. Basic canoe and safety instructions are included. Shuttle service is available for various sections of the Chestatee and Etowah Rivers. You can arrange for private guides. Ask about family and group discounts.

Appalachian Outfitters is open warm weekends (65° and over) in March and October, every day April through September, and other times by prior arrangement. The company is closed the third weekend in October and Easter Sunday.

Canoe-the-Hooch Outpost and Rentals
Route 4, Box 4548
Cleveland, GA 30528
706-865-5751
Contact: Larry Portwood

This company offers white-water canoeing on the Chattahoochee River. The Upper Section, with maximum Class II rapids, is ideal for beginner to intermediate paddlers. The Lower Section contains maximum Class III rapids and is suited for intermediate to advanced paddlers. Both trips are approximately six miles and take three to four hours. A day trip from Sautee Creek to Duncan Bridge, with maximum Class III rapids, is appropriate for intermediate and advanced paddlers. This trip is approximately fourteen miles and takes seven to eight hours. Rental fees for canoes and rafts are based on the number of people and the trip you choose; they include parking and shuttle. For reservations, write or call seven days a week.

Nantahala Outdoor Center
P.O. Box 1390
Clayton, GA 30525
800-232-7238

In business for twenty-one years, the center has guided over a million people downriver. Instruction is provided before and during each whole- or half-day guided white-water rafting trip. All river gear is provided, including high-quality rafts, paddles, life jackets, and helmets. In cool weather, wet suits are available at no extra cost. Lunch is provided on Section III and IV runs. You can even purchase photographs of your trip. The minimum age on Section III is ten years and thirteen on Section IV. A guide rides in every other raft when Section III waters are at moderate levels and in every raft when waters are extremely high or low. On Section IV, a guide rides in each raft. NOC also offers overnighters and custom programs. Reservations are required. Rates include a contribution to river conservation. Ask about off-season and group rates.

Highlights of the six-hour Section III run are Bull Sluice Rapids and calm pools that let you enjoy the mountainside lush with wildflowers. The seven-hour Section IV run climaxes at Five Falls, where the river thunders through constricting boulders and over steep drops. After all that excitement, you can get your adrenaline level back to normal during the leisurely paddle across Lake Tugaloo.

Southeastern Expeditions
2936-H North Druid Hills Road
Atlanta, GA 30329
800-868-RAFT; in Atlanta, 404-329-0433
Ocoee Outpost, 615-338-8073
Chattooga Outpost, 706-782-4331

Billed as "Where the Adventure Begins," this twenty-two-year-old company offers rafting, canoe, and kayak clinics on the Chattooga and the Ocoee. The range of activities guarantees something appropriate for the whole family and white-water enthusiasts from novices to the most experienced.

Section III raft trips consist of Class II and III rapids, including Bull Sluice and a Class IV falls. At moderate water levels, a guide accompanies every other raft. The minimum age is ten.

Section IV raft trips offer frequent steep drops and ledges as well as breathtaking waterfalls. At the end of the trip, a motorboat service pushes your raft across the two miles of Lake Tugaloo. The minimum age is thirteen.

The Deluxe Adventure is an overnight trip that rafts Section III and Bull Sluice the first day, followed by a camp-out in the natural wilderness. Section IV is run the second day. This trip includes two lunches, a steak or trout dinner, a hot breakfast, and camping gear—except for a sleeping bag and pad, which you must provide. The minimum age is thirteen.

Ocoee trips pass through five miles of Class III and IV waters and take about two hours. The minimum age is twelve.

A white-water photographer accompanies each trip. Photos are available for purchase at each outpost. Guides are CPR and first aid certified and participate in ongoing river rescue training programs.

All trips begin with an orientation talk. They are available most weekdays and during select weekends April through October. Reservations are required. A portion of your fee is donated to community service and a river conservation trust fund. Other services and packages include half-day Chattooga excursions; Saddle & Paddle, a horseback ride one day, followed by rafting the next; customized one- to three-day canoe/kayak outings on the upper Chattooga; day trips on Section II; personalized instruction; motorcoach charters; double-run packages; catered lunches; multitrip discounts; full food service; interpretive presentations, and a referral service for other rivers. In addition to the white-water activities, Southeastern Expeditions offers a rope course at the Chattooga Outpost.

Wildwater, Ltd.
P.O. Box 100
Long Creek, SC 29658
800-762-2463
Contact: Jim Greiner

With twenty-two years' experience under their belts, the folks at Wildwater offer eleven river trips for all ages and skills as well as a program called Raft and Rail, minitrips, and overnighters.

Wildwater's Ocoee trip is escorted by an experienced guide, making the trip suitable for beginners and experienced rafters. The rafting center features a campground, hot showers, a store, and a deli. Group meals are available with advance reservations. The trip takes about four hours. The minimum age is twelve. Trips are scheduled weekends March through May and September and October and daily except Tuesday and Wednesday from June through August.

A variety of trips on the Chattooga range from one-half day to two days. Trips are scheduled daily from March through October. The twenty-acre rafting center features Chauga River House, a bed and breakfast, as well as cabins, a lake, and full modern facilities.

The half-day minitrip operates weekdays only and is recommended for families, first-time rafters, and those who want a shorter, less strenuous trip. Choose from guided and self-guided rafts. The trip lasts about 4.5 hours, and snacks are served. The minimum age is eight.

Rafting section III involves a full-day trip that includes lunch and entails Class III and IV rapids. You can choose between guided and self-guided expeditions. The minimum age is ten. Section IV is the ultimate challenge. This section of the river drops many times more rapidly than the Grand Canyon. Larger guided rafts are used. The outing includes lunch. The minimum age is thirteen.

Raft the whole Chattooga on a two-day trip that features an overnight camp-out, a steak cookout, a full cooked breakfast, two lunches, and camping gear except for a sleeping bag. You can substitute a country inn or motel lodging for the camp-out at no extra cost. For both Section III and IV, the minimum age is thirteen.

Group rates are available for all trips. Reservations are highly recommended, as trips fill up well in advance. When you call, have several dates in mind.

The Raft and Rail program includes a two-hour excursion on the Great Smoky Mountain Railway through the Nantahala Gorge, followed by a seven-mile guided raft trip on the Nantahala. The trip includes a picnic lunch, hot showers, and change facilities. A special phone number set up for this program is 800-872-4681.

Wildewood Outpost
P. O. Box 999
Helen, GA 30545
800-553-2715 or 706-865-4451

Wildewood's motto is "Take only memories, leave only ripples, kill only time." The outfitter offers five- and ten-mile white-water canoe and raft trips for beginners and intermediates on the Chattahoochee River. You can rent rafts or canoes for a self-guided excursion or make arrangements for a guided trip. Shuttle service is provided at an additional cost. Reservations are preferred.

OTHER OUTFITTERS

Georgia Wildlife Adventures, Inc.
404-978-0624

Tim Zech offers a variety of adventures particularly popular with out-of-town visitors. He'll pick you up at your hotel, transport you to your chosen venture, provide you with all necessary equipment and accessories, then return you to your hotel.

Eagle Adventure Company
P.O. Box 970
McCaysville, GA 30555
800-288-3245

Kayak Day Trips
706-754-5885

Whitewater Express
1240 Clairmont Road
Decatur, GA 30030
800-676-7238

Whitewater Rafting
706-632-5680

Whitewater Rafting & Canoeing
800-334-7828

SEA KAYAKING

The kayak is one of the world's most ancient forms of transportation. While few people today use the kayak for survival, many enthusiasts have found kayaks to be a pleasurable means to enter remote areas not easily accessible any other way. Sea kayaks are somewhat different from their river-running brothers. They are harder to capsize because they are wider and have a broader base. Sea kayaks are easier to get in and out of and are easy to control with a rudder operated by foot pedals. Therefore, advanced paddling skills are not as necessary.

A sea kayaker must consider the current and the size of the waves. He or she should be able to use a compass and possess some minor navigational skills. Of course, once past breaking water, the sea kayaking experience is more like that of quiet-water kayaking.

Paddling on Georgia's coast is popular because you can explore salt marshes and barrier islands such as Cumberland Island National Seashore. You can paddle out to the island and go up streams to the interior.

Ocean Motion
1300 Ocean Boulevard
St. Simons, GA 31522
912-638-5225

This outfitter not only rents sea kayaks, but also provides guided tours.

ORGANIZATIONS

Atlanta Whitewater Club

P.O. Box 33
Clarkston, GA 30021
404-299-3752

The Atlanta Whitewater Club meets monthly. After the business meeting, members view videos on such topics as paddling or outdoor expeditions all over the world. The monthly newsletter highlights upcoming trips and other pertinent information.

The AWC hosts frequent trips led by qualified advanced paddlers, to Ocoee, Chattooga, Nantahala, and the Gauley in West Virginia.

The club holds outdoor rolling practice all summer. In the winter, practice is held in an indoor pool. Certified American Canoe Association instructors teach practice.

AWC also offers beginning, intermediate, and advanced paddling instruction. A two-day clinic emphasizes in-water time, eddy turns, strokes, ferries, surfing, and river reading. Other clinics include safety, CPR, paddle repair, and forward strokes.

The club sponsors several annual races, held off Powers Ferry Road on the short slalom course maintained by the club. In addition, AWC sponsors races on the Ocoee and Nantahala.

All summer, the club runs the "metro Hooch." Members gather for fun and relaxation as they paddle from Powers Ferry to US 41.

In the fall, the club holds its annual picnic that includes volleyball and water polo played from boats. Club members also gather for camping, hiking, skiing, and other outdoor events. A member of the American Canoe Association, the club is dedicated to conservation and preservation of the natural environment and improved access to rivers.

Georgia Canoeing Association
P.O. Box 7023
Atlanta, GA 30357
404-421-9729
(See Chapter 7 for more
  details on this club.)

Paddle Georgia
Central Georgia River
  Runners
P.O. Box 6563
Macon, GA 31208
912-477-5530
Contact: Dick Creswell

INSTRUCTION

Medicine Bow
Route 8, Box 1780/Wahsega Road
Dahlonega, GA 30533
706-864-5928

Mark Warren, four-time Dixie Division Open Canoe Slalom Champion, offers private instruction through his primitive school of earthlore in the North Georgia mountains.

MISCELLANEOUS

For information on water levels, call the TVA Water Resources Line, 800-238-2264.

Special Events

The Nantahala Outdoor Center sponsors several events, such

as the Perception Citizen Race Series, the Ocoee World Cup Slalom, Outdoorsman's Triathlon, and the Guest Appreciation Festival and Used Equipment Sale.

Bibliography

Boyd, Brian. *The Chattooga Wild and Scenic River.* Clayton, GA: Ferncreek Publisher, 1994.

Estes, Carter and Almquist. *Canoe Trails of the Deep South.* Birmingham, AL: Menasha Ridge Press, 1993.

Sehlinger, Bob. *Paddlers' Guide to North Georgia.* Birmingham, AL: Menasha Ridge Press, 1993.

10

SOMETHING
FOR EVERYONE

The sports covered in the preceding chapters may not have struck your fancy, or perhaps you're burned out on them. Other outdoor activity possibilities are as limitless as your imagination.

Many of the following sports have small local chapters run by volunteers that change from year to year, so they may have only a post office box—no street address or phone number. If we have not listed a contact, check the newspaper *Creative Loafing,* the magazine *Atlanta Sports & Fitness,* or at a local shop where equipment for that activity is sold for the most current person to contact.

AIR DOGFIGHTS

Sky Warriors
3996 Aviation Circle

Suite B-3
Fulton County—Brown Field
Atlanta, GA 30336
404-699-7000

Shades of Snoopy and the Red Baron—updated. Or the ultimate virtual-reality video game. You can participate in an aerial battle and walk away from it. You'll fly in a two-seater T-34A military trainer (used by the Air Force in the 1950s) with an experienced fighter pilot. You don't have to have a pilot's license as long as you are sixteen or older and in good health.

The adventure begins with a ninety-minute preflight briefing in military style as if you were going out on an actual mission. Then two or three planes go up. During the dogfight phase, you actually fly the aircraft. Each plane is equipped with a laser cannon that simulates a 50-mm machine gun. If you score a "hit" on another plane, a smoke burst is emitted. Three videocameras on board document your flight. Once back on the ground, you can analyze your skills, and you get to keep the tape.

Sky Warriors normally offers two flights per day during the week and three per day on the weekends. An annual contest pits former participants against each other.

ARCHERY

Medicine Bow, Ltd.
Route 4, Box 1342, Wahsega Road
Dahlonega, GA 30533
706-864-5928
Contact: Mark Warren

Medicine Bow offers archery instruction for all ages, summer camps for kids, camps for adults, and many special events and competitions, such as two medieval events—Robin and Maid Marion May Day Tournament and Robin O' the Hood Day. A three-day workshop teaches you how to make a Cherokee-style bow of hickory or locust wood. In addition, Medicine Bow offers a Parent-Child Native American Weekend throughout the year, nature walks, and canoe trips.

Henry County Archery Association
Contact Ann-Marie Patterson, 404-474-3345, or Jerry Richardson, 404-483-4415.

Meeting monthly, the association welcomes members from the age of four. The 100-member club encourages family memberships. Practice is held on a fifty-acre tract using traditional and McKenzie targets such as life-size bear, turkey, elk, and deer. In addition to shooting from standard distances, a course set up in the woods creates realistic situations where participants must shoot from unknown distances.

BEACH SPORTS

Barry's Beach Service
P.O. Box 1757
St. Simons, GA 31522
912-638-8053

With locations at both the King & Prince Hotel and the Beach Club Condominiums, Barry's can provide whatever you need for a fun-filled day at the beach—sailboats (including Hobie Cats), sea kayaks, sailboards, and rafts as well as lessons and rides. Barry's also offers bikes, Windsurfer rentals, chairs, and umbrellas. Rentals are by the hour, half-day, or full day.

Ocean Motion
1300 Ocean Boulevard
St. Simons, GA 31522
912-638-5225

In addition to renting rollerblades and bikes, Ocean Motion sells bikes, sportswear, kayaks, Hobie Cats, surfboards, boogie boards, and rollerblades. The company conducts two- and four-hour river and ocean kayak tours.

BIRD WATCHING

Larry Kennedy Charters
   (marsh cruises for bird enthusiasts)
Hampton Club Marina
St. Simons, GA 31522
912-638-3214

Salt Marsh Boat Ride
Sea Island Fishing Dock
Sea Island, GA 31561
912-638-3611, extension 5202, or 638-9354
Contact: Jim and Jeanne Pleasants

A trained naturalist who has also served seven years as fishing guide conducts narrated tours of the salt marsh. Other tours include shelling and nature tours. All tours also cover the history of area.

Okefenokee Swamp Park
Waycross, GA 31501
912-283-0583

This nonprofit organization operates under a long-term lease and is separate from the Okefenokee National Wildlife Refuge. However, it is a wildlife sanctuary and features a Serpentarium and Wildlife Observatory; the Swamp Creation Center, highlighting the history of the "land of the trembling earth"; and a Living Swamp Center with a live deer observatory. The general admission price includes a guided boat tour deep into the swamp. A boardwalk leads to an observation tower. Frequent interpretive exhibits, lectures, and wildlife shows keep folks coming back. There are no night activities, camping, or overnight accommodations.

BUNGEE JUMPING

Dixie Land Fun Park
1675 North State 85
Fayetteville, GA 30214
404-460-5862 or 460-9941

CORPORATE CHALLENGES
(For specific information, refer to the categories listed below.)

- **The Challenge Rock Climbing School**—rock climbing/ rapelling
- **Medicine Bow**—survival skills
- **Southeastern Expeditions**—ropes challenge
- **Wolfcreek Wilderness School**—survival skills

DISABLED

Georgia Handicapped Sportsmen
5865-D Oakbrook Parkway
Norcross, GA 30093
404-246-9810

This organization is a nonprofit group of individuals with physical disabilities. Its stated purpose is "to promote friendship, fellowship, mutual understanding and cooperation among handicapped people by encouraging them to participate in outdoor sports." Regularly scheduled events include deer and turkey hunts, dove shoots, skeet and trap shoots, and bass tournaments.

Fishing

Coastal fishing areas with handicapped access include the Frank W. Spencer Recreational Park, Lazaretto Creek Pier on the Tybee Island Causeway, Tybee Island Pier on Tybee Beach, Tivoli River Park Fishing Docks, Riceboro River Bridge Fishing Dock, Champney River Park Catwalk, Blythe Island Regional Park Fishing Pier, Jekyll Island Pier, St. Simons Pier, Harriett's Bluff, and Woodbine Recreational Park.

Several of Georgia's State Parks and Historic Sites and Corps of Engineers lakes Walter F. George and West Point Lake have handicapped access.

Horseback Riding

Crawford Center for Therapeutic Horsemanship
Chastain Park

4371 Powers Ferry Road, N.W.
Atlanta, GA 30327-3416
404-257-1470
Contact: Shirley Crawford

This center provides therapeutic riding for 100 riders per week by doctor's prescription. Participants have a wide range of emotional and/or physical handicaps. A series of eight one-hour group lessons is offered during the spring, summer, and fall. English hunt seat is taught and all lessons are in the ring. There are no trail rides or rentals.

The Good Shepherd Riding Academy, Inc.
Bar Rest Ranch
Warm Springs, GA 31830
706-655-2354

Good Shepherd, affiliated with North American Riding for the Handicapped, provides therapeutic horseback riding for the mentally and physically disabled. Nestled on the side of picturesque Pine Mountain, the academy is adjacent to the Roosevelt Warm Springs Institute for Rehabilitation and the Franklin D. Roosevelt State Park and was once part of the largest dude ranch in the Southeast. President Roosevelt enjoyed riding horseback around the Little White House. Today the ranch offers classroom and hands-on experiences; a covered arena and mounting area; a petting zoo and other activities such as hayrides, cookouts, trail rides, and participation in parades and Special Olympics competition. There are no charges to individual students.

Winship Ayon Center, Inc. also provides therapeutic riding.
Sweet Sunshine Farm

1675 Thompson Road
Alpharetta, GA 30201
404-475-8319

Hiking/Nature Trails

Lakeshore Trail in the Chestatee Ranger District of the Chattahoochee National Forest encircles Dockery Lake and is accessible to the disabled.

Marshall Forest—Braille Trail
404-291-0766

Marshall Forest is Georgia's first National Natural Landmark. The 250-acre primeval woodland includes the specially designed trail for the visually impaired.

Adaptive Sports

Fulton County Parks and Recreation
1575 Northside Drive, N.W.
Atlanta, GA 30318
404-730-6200

    South Fulton Therapeutics at Cliftondale Park (4399 Butner Road, College Park, GA 30349) offers recreational programs for special populations year-round. These activities consist of indoor/outdoor recreational games, athletic events, arts and crafts, physical fitness, and cultural and educational field trips for youth and adults. All programs emphasize motor skill development, socialization, and self-image enhancement. Special Olympics training is offered to appropriate participants. Contact David Bailey or Thomas Hughes at 404-306-3061.

Special Recreational Services Center (6005 Glenridge Drive, Atlanta, GA 30328) offers recreational programs for normal and special populations year-round, including senior citizens, mentally handicapped youth, autistic youth, behavior-disordered youth, learning-disabled youths, and high-risk youths. Contact Robin Steiner, Cathy Bell, or Spencer Davis, Recreational Therapists, at 404-303-6181.

Georgia Chapter of the Multiple Sclerosis Society
1100 Circle 75 Parkway
Atlanta, GA 30339
404-984-9080

This chapter sponsors aquatic exercise classes at various YMCAs. The society also suggests contacting your parks and recreation department to see if they offer any adaptive sports.

Shepherd Spinal Clinic
2020 Peachtree Road, N.W.
Atlanta, GA 30309-1465
404-350-7375

Shepherd Spinal Clinic organizes adaptive sports primarily for people with spinal injuries or neurological diseases that affect coordination. However, the clinic arranges outpatient activities for any disability. Sports include hunting, fishing, rafting, canoeing, kayaking, camping, scuba diving, jet skiing, waterskiing. An adaptive devices specialist aids in equipment modifications that range from a firing mechanism to pull a trigger to electric reels for fishing rods. One camping, one hunting, and one fishing outing are planned each month. An annual camp called Adventure Skills Workshop, held at handicapped accessible campsites, concentrates on water sports.

Shepherd Spinal Clinic provides a different specialist for each outdoor program. Call 404-352-2020 to reach individual program directors. The clinic arranges for disabled people to participate in the Crawford Center for Therapeutic Horsemanship (see above).

Camping

Will-A-Way Recreation Area
404-867-5313

Located within Fort Yargo State Park, the special-purpose recreation area is designed for the disabled and features a group facility capable of serving 200.

FRISBEE

More frisbees are sold each year than baseballs, basketballs, and footballs combined. Numerous disc sports have evolved, as have competitions. You can purchase discs, get tips on perfecting your skills, and get information on clubs and competitions from the Little Five Points shop:

Identified Flying Objects
1164 Euclid Avenue
Atlanta, GA 30307
404-524-4628

Disc golf was developed as an organized sport in 1969 using trees and lampposts as targets. In 1976, the flying disc entrapment device, called the pole-hole, was invented, and the first permanent course was developed. There are now over 500 permanent courses nationwide. One shot is counted each time the disc is thrown or a penalty is incurred. The object is to acquire the lowest score in a round of eighteen holes. The game demands a wide range of throwing skills, including distance and accuracy and control of curves, hovers, rollers, and skips. Georgia courses include:

Blackburn Disc Golf Course, Dahlonega, 706-864-4050
Rosewood—DeKalb Disc Golf Course, Lithonia (no phone)
Oregon Park, Marietta, 404-528-8899
Wills Park, Alpharetta, 404-740-2414

Greater Atlanta Dog and Disc Club
Peter Bloeme
4060-D Peachtree Road, Suite 326
Atlanta, GA 30319
404-231-9240

The club was founded by Jeff Perry and his dog, Gilbert, who have performed in the United States and Europe, as well as appearing on CNN and the "Today Show." They were inducted into the Ashley Whippet Hall of Fame after winning the 1992 World Finals. In addition to competitions, members perform at various fairs, festivals, and charity functions. Membership includes the newsletter "The Fire Hydrant."

Atlanta Flying Disc Club,
404-612-8248,
Contact: Chris O'Cleary

AFDC sponsors a frisbee team sport called Vitimate. Co-ed summer and winter leagues alternate with tournament play throughout the Southeast in the fall and spring.

171

GLIDING

Soaring enthusiasts liken the sport to a combination of sailing, surfing, and skiing. The popular sport requires no previous flying instruction, and participants can solo as young as age fourteen.

Atlanta Soaring Club
P.O. Box 337
Kingston, GA 30145
404-336-5006

Based at the Etowah Bend Airport in Northwest Georgia, this club provides the opportunity to enjoy the sensations of silent flight aboard a sailplane. An added bonus is a bird's-eye view of the beautiful Etowah River Valley.The airport is open to the public for demonstration flights on Saturdays, Sundays, and major holidays throughout the year. Flights can be scheduled by appointment on weekdays. Flights last about thirty-five minutes. Anyone interested in gliding can join the club. The club, which meets bimonthly, promotes camps, cookouts, races, promotional events, and work parties.

Mid-Georgia Soaring Association
Charles Dewald
5428 Pheasant Run
Stone Mountain, GA 30087
404-621-0522

This nonprofit organization operates from the Walton County Airport in Central Georgia. It sponsors regional and national contests, mountain flying camps, air shows, and social events.

The club owns four aircraft and will soon offer sailplane flight instruction.

HANG GLIDING

Georgia Hang Gliding Association
c/o United States Hang Gliding Association
Colorado Springs, CO 80933
719-632-8300

The state record for hang gliding was 154 miles from Lookout Mountain to Interstate 20. In addition to the commercial facility at Lookout Mountain, the GHGA has researched and obtained approval for using seven other locations—Kurlee Mountain, John Mountain, Menlo Mountain, Pigeon Mountain near LaFayette, Rising Fawn, Mount Yonah, and Bell Mountain. The organization meets monthly. The purpose is to identify more sites, encourage more people to participate in the sport, and to develop other means of hang gliding, such as truck towing. GHGA is a member of the U.S. Hang Gliding Association. The national organization issues licenses, teaches courses, certifies instructors, and rates sites. Contact Tom Bell at 404-751-9263.

Lookout Mountain Flight Park & Training Center
Route 2, Box 215-H, Dept. HF
Rising Fawn, GA 30738
800-688-LMFP or 706-398-3541

Certified instructors take you on your first flights on their grassy, gently sloping "bunny hill." Your eventual goal will be soaring from world-famous Lookout Mountain. Open all year, the center provides lessons every day, for which all equipment is supplied. Easy step-by-step instructions let you learn at your own pace. Package plans and group rates are available. The center also features camping, swimming, and mountain bikes.

Special events throughout the year include Aero Towing Clinics, Antique/Classic Hang Gliding Meet, the Lookout Mountain Aerobatic Hang Gliding Competition, and the Airwave Vision Classic Hang Gliding Competition.

Hang Glider Heaven
Seed Tick Road and Highway 441
Clayton, GA 30525
706-782-6218 or 782-9908

Unless you are experienced enough to participate in competition, Hang Glider Heaven is more for spectators than for participants. The organization sponsors several hang-gliding events and air shows each year. A game preserve is also located on the grounds. Accommodations are available in rental cabins.

Cloudbase
Route 1, Box 240
Wildwood, GA 30757
706-820-2017

Southern Air Time Inc.
2475 Pruett Road
Duluth, GA 30136
404-476-5446

HOT-AIR BALLOONING

Head Balloons
P.O. Box 28

Helen, GA 30545
706-865-3874 or 865-6565
Contact: Craig McDonald

When you want information on balloon rides, competitions, or purchases, go straight to the horse's mouth—in this case the only hot-air balloon manufacturer in Georgia and one of only six in the country. Head Balloons offers hour to hour-and-half champagne rides for two to four people by appointment.

Aeronautical Enterprises
2868A Lanora Road
Snellville, GA 30278
404-972-1741

**Atlanta Hot Air
Promotions**
5455 Buford Highway
Doraville, GA 30340
404-452-0033

Bulldawg Balloon Tours
Atlanta and Athens
404-389-8981

Hot Air Balloon Place
404-949-2424

**Peach Blossom
Balloons Inc.**
2749 Tritt Springs Drive,
   N.E.
Marietta, GA 30062
404-565-9023

**Southeastern Balloon
Services**
1815 Britt Road
Snellville, GA 30278
404-985-8079

**Georgia Balloon
Association**
P.O. Box 47747
Atlanta, GA 30362

Special Events

Gwinnett County will host the 1995-1997 U.S. Hot Air Balloon Team Championships. The ten-day event involves 100

175

professional balloonists competing in teams of three, as well as 100 amateur balloonists and 600 crew members. Over 500,000 spectators are expected. Organizers hope to gain consideration of hot-air ballooning as a future Olympic sport.

Annual festivals are held in Helen, Macon, Atlanta, and Valdosta.

LLAMA TREKKING

Hawksbell Farm
1618 Dawnville Road
Dalton, GA 30721
706-259-9310

Hike the beautiful Chattahoochee National Forest in the company of llamas. Bring your cameras and a big appetite; lunch is provided, along with hammocks for an afternoon rest. Hikers lead the llamas, who carry the gear. Hikes can be customized from two to six hours and are available any day of the week. Group and family rates are available.

Eagle Adventure Company
P.O. Box 970
McCaysville, GA 30555
800-288-3245

NATURE WALKS/TRIPS

Augusta Canal Authority
801 Broad Street, Room 507
Augusta, GA 30901
706-722-1071

As you walk, bike, or canoe along the canal, you'll enjoy the abundant plants that thrive along the canal, including giant loblolly pines, cypress, winged elm, sugarberry, sweet gum, patch-barked sycamore, and oak. In the trees you'll see mistletoe and Spanish moss.

At the water's edge, you'll find submerged and semi-submerged water plants such as elodea, parrot feather, bulrushes, and cattails. Creepers include trumpet creeper vine, honeysuckle, and, unfortunately, poison ivy.

Wildlife includes kingfishers, geese, osprey, beaver, river otter, deer, wild turkey, bald eagle, wood stork, great blue heron, green heron, loons, banded water snakes, yellow-bellied slider turtles, alligators, bobcats, cotton-mouth moccasins, and raccoons.

Autrey Mill Nature Preserve
9770 Autrey Mill Road
Alpharetta, GA 30202
404-664-0660

The twenty-seven-acre site showcases natural scenic beauty, a stream corridor, wildlife, and several historically interesting farm buildings as well as the ruins of Autrey Mill and Dam, which date back to the 1800s. The former miller's home houses the Autrey Mill Nature Preserve Association as well as the Autrey Mill Nature Center.

Birdsong Nature Center
Route 3, Box 1077
Thomasville, GA 31792
912-377-4408

This 565-acre tract was originally Birdsong Plantation and

was worked from the 1850s to 1930s by four generations of the William Dickey family. Betty and Ed Komarek purchased the land in 1938 and used controlled burning and other land-management techniques to transform the overworked farm into a haven for wildlife. Birdsong is now a nature center of habitat and wildlife diversity. Of special note are the Bird Window, where visitors can learn to identify birds up close; and the Listening Place, where they can observe the Big Bay Swamp and its critters. The center is open to the public several days a week. You need to call for days of operation because they vary.

Callaway Gardens
P.O. Box 2000
Pine Mountain, GA 31822
800-282-8181

The Discovery Trail offers 7.5 miles of leisurely touring through the Garden's natural areas. You can access the trail from numerous locations. It meanders past the Day Butterfly Center, the Log Cabin, the Ida Cason Callaway Memorial Chapel, Mr. Cason's Vegetable Garden, and the Sibley Horti-cultural Center, as well as through wooded areas and by streams and lakes. A ferry is available at the boat dock to transport riders across Mountain Creek Lake.

Chattahoochee Nature Center, Inc.
9135 Willeo Road
Roswell, GA 30075
404-992-2055

Nestled along the banks of the Chattahoochee River, just north of metro Atlanta, the environmental education facility is an oasis of wooded uplands, freshwater ponds, and marshes with miles of nature walks. The center also provides activity rooms, live animal displays, Nature Store, guest artists, classes, field trips, and seasonal activities at such times as Halloween and Easter. There is a small admission charge.

Cochran Mill Park
6875 Cochran Mill Road
Palmetto, GA 30268
404-463-6304

This 800-acre facility offers miles of pristine nature trails, waterfalls, wildlife, and an abundance of wildflowers. Visitors can picnic, hike, or go horseback riding. Group camping is available by reservation. A ranger station is located on the site.

Medicine Bow
Route 4, Box 1342
Wahsega Road
Dahlonega, GA 30533
706-864-5928

Special events include Fall Weekend with the Earth, an in-depth study of the autumn plants of Southern Appalachia, and how to identify and use them as food, medicine, and crafts. Tracking and Stalking teaches gaits, prints, and track patterns.Winter Weekend with the Earth includes a study of leafless plants and fire.

Salt Marsh Nature Tour
Inland Charter Boat Service
North First Street

P.O. Box 11
Sea Island, GA 31561
912-638-3611, ext. 5202
Contact: Frank and Janet Mead

This leisurely pontoon-boat ride through tidal creeks and salt marsh is guided by docents accredited by University of Georgia Marine Extension Service. The 105-minute tour provides close-up glimpses of plants and creatures of the salt marsh, including wading birds and osprey, as well as bottlenose dolphins, mink, and otter. The company also offers bird watching and shelling excursions to Pelican Spit. Cruises depart from the Sea Island dock for daylight, evening, and sunset voyages.

Cumberland Island National Seashore
P.O. Box 806
St. Marys, GA 31558
912-882-4337
(See Chapter 11)

Jekyll Island Wharf
#1 Pier Road
Jekyll Island, GA 31520
912-635-2891

Join a Dolphin Watch and spend two hours searching for the creatures and observing the shrimp fleet in action. This jaunt is great for camera buffs.

Kayak Nature Tours
Ocean Motion
1300 Ocean Boulevard

St. Simons, GA 31522
912-638-5225

Coastal islands, marsh creeks, and secluded beaches are easily accessible by stable touring kayaks. The two-hour guided tour includes an introductory instructional clinic.

Okefenokee National Wildlife Refuge
Route 2, Box 338
Folkston, GA 31537
912-496-3331

Guided one- and two-hour boat tours are ideal for bird watching, nature study, and photography. In addition, you can rent a boat for a self-guided tour.

Sapelo Island National Estuarine Sanctuary Tours
McIntosh County Chamber of Commerce
P.O. Box 1497
Darien, GA 31305
912-437-6684

After a thirty-minute ferry ride to the island, the guided tour includes salt marsh ecosystems, beach dunes, and maritime forests as well as the University of Georgia Marine Research Institute. In addition, you'll see Hog Hammock, one of the few surviving sites on the Atlantic seaboard of ethnic African-American culture; Behaviour Cemetery, a still-used cemetery originally for slaves; Long Tabby, a former sugar boiling house; South End House, a restored plantation home; Sapelo Lighthouse, Nannygoat Beach, Cabretta Island, Raccoon Bluff, Chocolate, Shell Ring, High Point, and Bourbon. Reservations are required. You can buy tickets at the Chamber or at the Welcome Center at 105 Fort King George Drive, 404-437-4192.

Spartina Trails
P.O. Box 2531
Savannah, GA 31402
912-234-4621

Spartina Trails offers exploration of Georgia's barrier islands. You can eavesdrop on the underwater conversations of dolphins and other sea creatures using hydrophones. Other activities include hiking onshore, bird watching along the coast, and fishing using a seine net.

Wilderness Southeast
711 Sandtown Road
Savannah, GA 31410
912-897-5108
(See Chapters 2 and 12)

Warwoman Dell Nature Trail
Tallulah Ranger District
Chattahoochee National Forest
Chechero/Savannah Street
P.O. Box 438
Clayton, GA 30525
706-632-3031

This volunteer-built trail in Northeastern Georgia offers a half-mile nature walk. Signs along the trail identify many common plants and the role they play in the environment.

OFF-ROAD VEHICLES

In the Chattahoochee-Oconee National Forests, several trails are designated for use by off-road vehicles (ORVs), which may include motorbikes or all-terrain vehicles (ATVs).

These trails include: **Houston Valley, Nottely Lake, Beasley Knob, Locust Stake, Anderson Creek, Whissenhant, Barnes Creek, Tatum Lead, Tibbs, Oakey Mountain, Brawley Mountain,** and **Town Creek.**

Even though you are not on the state's highways, to drive on these trails you must be of legal age to obtain a Georgia drivers license or be accompanied by a licensed driver. State laws and regulations apply concerning operation of a motor vehicle, and that includes not operating a motor vehicle under the influence of alcohol or drugs. Unless your vehicle has working headlights and taillights, don't ride between one-half hour after sunset to one-half hour before sunrise. Stay on ORV-designated trails, roads, and areas.

The U.S. Forest Service recommends that you follow these safety rules: wear boots, helmets, gloves, and eye protection to fend off twigs, flying rocks, and mud; be in good physical condition and be prepared to walk out in case of breakdown; make sure your vehicle—particularly the brakes—is in good condition; know how to make simple repairs and carry tools with you; don't race; adjust your speed to fit the situation; obey all posted rules. Try not to create excessive smoke and noise.

For more information, contact the Forest Supervisor at:

U.S. Forest Service
508 Oak Street, N.W.

Gainesville, GA 30501
404-536-0541

RACEWALKING

Walking Club of Georgia
4920 Roswell Road, Suite 123
Atlanta, GA 30342
404-847-WALK
Contact: Bonnie Stein

The statewide organization is geared to three walking methods: fitness walking, racewalking, and hiking. Most members have taken a racewalking to fitness course or are competitive racewalkers. Racewalking has been an Olympic event since 1908, and participants use Olympic methods and rules. The club is open to all ages. In fact, current members range from eight to ninety. The monthly newsletter includes a statewide racing calendar, information on events and fitness walks, and tips on purchasing discount gear and clothing. If you're interested in racewalking, contact Ace Walkers through the club. Ace Walkers offers classes all over the metro area as well as a few statewide. There are many other small racewalking clubs around the state.

REENACTMENTS

They come from all over and from all walks of life—men, women, and children, from brain surgeons to taxi drivers—to provide living-history lessons about the Civil War. They supply their own costumes and equipment and live in tents and cook simple meals over open fires, just as their ancestors did. Some participants travel to a reenactment every weekend of the year. Some are lucky enough to work as extras in movies and TV shows about the historical period.

The most complete listing of units and reenactments for the Civil War period is the *Civil War Times Gazette*. Many reenactments are associated with national or state parks such as Andersonville, Resaca, Chickamauga, and Kennesaw Mountain as well as the Atlanta History Center.

While we are well-acquainted with Civil War reenactments, we didn't know that other people and units have chosen to reenact such periods as the Revolutionary War. One group is even staging commemorative reenactments for World Wars I and II. Revolutionary War events in Georgia include Fort Morris (south of Savannah) in February, a living-history event at Elijah Clark State Park in March, and a similar event at Nancy Hart State Park in May.

Participants have a good network for informing each other when events are planned, but there is no comprehensive list, and the exact dates vary from year to year. To learn about when and where interpretations, encampments, and reenactments will be staged, contact the park or area you are interested in or the local visitors bureau.

ROCK/SPORT CLIMBING

Climbing expert/instructor/author Chris Watford of Call of the Wild in Roswell has climbed all over the country, but he contends that some of the best climbing anywhere is found in the Southeast. Exceptional Georgia sites include Mt. Yonah, Tallulah Gorge (for experts), Curahee, Pigeon Mountain, and Lookout Mountain. Look for Watford's book, *The Southeast*

Climbers Home Companion/A Climbers Guide to Tennessee, Alabama and Georgia.

Atlanta Climbing Club
Atlanta, GA
404-621-5070

The Atlanta Climbing Club promotes enjoyable, safe, and environmentally responsible climbing in all forms. Although the club does not offer instruction, it conducts monthly meetings on such topics as first aid and also sponsors numerous outings. A recorded message notifies the climbing community about meetings, events, and trips. ACA is open to anyone over eighteen.

Call of the Wild
425 Market Place
Roswell, GA 30075
404-992-5400

This outfitter was ahead of its time in offering climbing equipment even before the sport became so popular. You can arrange for instruction; there are no regularly scheduled classes.

The Challenge Rock Climbing School
1085 Capital Club Circle
Atlanta, GA 30319
404-237-4021

"Climb for the smile of it" is the motto of this school, which offers instruction in rock climbing/rappelling for all skill levels. Courses are taught at various locations. In addition to private lessons, you can choose from one-day accelerated courses in basic or level II skills, weekend courses, such as Introduction to Lead Climbing, Getting Started, or Advancing on the Rock, as well as a six-day summer camp. Experienced guides are available to take advanced groups to climbing sites. Early-bird discounts are available. The school provides all technical gear, such as ropes, harnesses, carabineers, and climbing shoes.

Director Jerry Dodgen is a rock climber, hang glider, and mountain biker. He stresses that climbing is about partnership, teamwork, and trust, making the sport ideal for corporate challenges. Periodically, the school gives free climbing clinics at the REI camping equipment store in Atlanta.

Eagle Adventure Company
P.O. Box 970
McCaysville, GA 30555
800-288-3245

The Sporting Club at Windy Hill
135 Interstate North Parkway
Atlanta, GA 30339
404-953-1100

This membership club is the only facility in the South with an artificial wall. Instructors offer lessons for kids and adults of any experience level. Beginning climbers are secured with special harnesses and are top-roped for safety. In addition to recreational climbing, the club sponsors challenge events.

You can reserve the club for rock climbing parties, using the artificial wall. The fee per person includes all equipment, instruction, and lunch.

Providence Outdoor Recreation Center
13440 Providence Park Drive
Alpharetta, GA 30201
404-740-2419

This unit of Fulton County Parks and Recreation teaches courses in basic rappelling and basic rock climbing as well as other outdoor skills such as backpacking and map and compass skills.

ROPES CHALLENGE

Southeastern Expeditions
2936-H North Druid Hills Road
Atlanta, GA 30329
800-868-RAFT or in Atlanta, 404-329-0433
Ocoee Outpost, 615-338-8073
Chattooga Outpost, 706-782-4331

Hidden away in the backwoods of the Chattooga Outpost is a maze of cables, ropes, and obstacles. Collectively called a team challenge or ropes course, it is ideally suited for groups seeking skills that increase self-confidence and develop the mutual support and trust necessary for team building. The course is available for groups of ten or more. It is divided into ground-level group-initiative activities and above-ground self-confidence portions. Content can be varied from a one-day course with lunch included to multiday challenges including rope work, seminars, and canoeing. The minimum age for participation is twelve.

ROWING/SCULLING

Rowing provides both strength and endurance training. With normal rowing, an athlete can burn up to 700 calories per hour, depending on intensity. While the exercise is low impact, the whole body is involved, because while you are pulling with your arms, you are also pushing with your legs and swinging with your body.

There are two types of rowing—sweeps (where each person has an oar on alternate sides and they row in unison) and sculling (where each person has two oars).

As the sport has increased in popularity, many high schools and colleges have added it to their sports programs either as a club or as a varsity sport. The University of Georgia, Georgia Tech, and the College of Art and Design in Savannah as well as eight high schools in the Atlanta area take part in the sport. Rowing clubs can be found in Augusta and Gainesville (which will be the 1996 Olympic venue).

Atlanta Rowing Club
500 Azalea Drive
Roswell, GA 30075
404-993-1879

Founded in 1974, this club is located at the Chattahoochee River Park just south of Roswell, where it maintains two boathouses and a pavilion as well as boats of both types in all sizes, from eight-man shells down to singles. You can also store private boats there. In addition, the club provides fitness equipment and specialized rowing training equipment.

From the clubhouse, the river is rowable for 1.5 miles

upstream to the Georgia 400 bridge and for 4 miles downstream to the Morgan Falls Dam. The average current is less than two knots. The surrounding cliffs provide a natural windbreak as well as a dramatic setting for rowing.

The club's very active youth program, the Atlanta Junior Rowing Association, teaches high school students, conducts interschool meets, and hosts the Georgia Tech Rowing Club.

Two major annual events are the **Head of the Chattahoochee Rowing Regatta** during the first weekend in November and the **Atlanta Rowing Festival** in the spring.

RUNNING

Atlanta Track Club
3097 East Shadowlawn Avenue, N.E.
Atlanta, GA 30305
404-231-9064 or the racing hotline 404-262-RACE

The best source of running information is the Atlanta Track Club, which operates a permanent office open five days a week. ATC is the largest track and road racing organization in the state. The world-renowned Peachtree Road Race, run on July 4, is the club's biggest yearly undertaking. The club offers a full range of track and field events for all ages and abilities on Tuesday evenings, May through July. The ATC Volunteer Coaching Program matches volunteer coaches with members based on geographical location and goals and abilities. Races are open to members and nonmembers. Team's include Women's Open and Masters, Men's Open (under 40), Men's Masters (40+), and Masters Track and Field (30+). ATC keeps information on statewide competitions and other clubs, most of which are run by volunteers. The monthly newsletter is called "The Wingfoot." Membership includes free entry into many races.

Other clubs include:

Chattahoochee Road Runners
P.O. Box 724745
Atlanta, GA 31139-1745
404-916-2790

Greater Gwinnett Road Runners
P.O. Box 1497
Snellville, GA 30278
404-979-5087

Helenboch Hoofers Running Club
P.O. Box 29464
Atlanta, GA 30359
404-986-8505

as well as **Atlanta Hash House Harriers, Atlanta Singles Running Organization, Cherokee Running Club,** and **Paulding Pacesetters Running Club.**

Life College Running Camp
1269 Barclay Circle
Marietta, GA 30060
404-424-0554, ext. 327

The world-class running course includes manmade fifty-foot sand dunes and a five-mile cross-country track. All ages can attend. Participants learn methods, techniques, and disciplines to maximize their running enjoyment. One fee includes instruction and meals. The camp is limited to forty participants.

SCUBA DIVING

A scuba workout has benefits similar to those of swimming, although diving doesn't really work the arm muscles. Legs, however, get a great workout. In addition to the actual dive, participants get another workout lugging their equipment— an air tank weighs about thirty-five pounds, and a weight belt weighs about fifteen pounds.

Gray's Reef off Sapelo

Gray's reef is the state's only natural marine habitat of this type. Located seventeen nautical miles east of Sapelo Island, the reef features sponges, hard coral, gorgonions, bryozoans, tropical fish, and dolphins.

Atlanta Reef Dwellers SCUBA Club

Created in 1971, this club teaches classroom coursework leading up to all levels of scuba diving certification. Instructors make regular trips to dive sites for actual certification. Popular sites around the state include free-water or ocean diving at Gray's Reef or one of the artificial reefs created by DNR, the most popular of which is a Liberty ship off Jekyll Island. Georgia scuba enthusiasts also dive in the Savannah River, where they find Civil War artifacts, and in the Chattahoochee River, quarries, and some lakes. In addition, there are some natural springs and caves in South Georgia.

SKATING/IN-LINE

The new roller blades have caused a revolution in roller skating, elevating it from circling a rink to a touring and racing sport. A well-trained skater can average 20 mph on long-distance tours and can reach downhill speeds of over 40 mph. Many runners and cyclists also use skating for cross-training purposes.

Atlanta Peachtree Roadrollers
1077 Vistavia Circle
Decatur, GA 30033
404-634-9032
Contact: Henry Zuver

"We don't write, we skate," said Valerie Zuver—with tongue in cheek—when we asked if the club had any written material. Obviously this is a group that takes its sport seriously while still having fun. One evening we were driving on Piedmont Road in Atlanta near the Abbey and the Mansion restaurants, and the Peachtree Roadrunners passed us—going uphill. To them, it was just another casual evening get-together. The club skates twice a week, on Monday and Wednesday evenings. The state organization boasts over 1,000 members.

SKIING

Atlanta Ski Club
6303 Barfield Road, Suite 120
Atlanta, GA 30328
404-255-4800

Surprisingly for a Southern city, Atlanta boasts one of the largest ski clubs in the country. The club sponsors ski trips to slopes in the Southeast, the West, and occasionally to Europe. In addition to an annual swap meet, the club sponsors many year-round social activities.

Sky Valley Resort
Box 39
Sky Valley, GA 30537
706-746-5301

Sky Valley is the only ski slope in Georgia. All it needs is cold temperatures to be able to use the snow-making equipment. Four ski slopes and a bunny hill range from 400 feet to 2,000 feet long. A double chairlift and tow-rope service all slopes.

SKYDIVING

Advances in equipment and training have made this popular sport easier and more accessible for would-be participants. Those who love the sport swear by the freedom, exhilaration, and tranquility of leaving an airplane thousands of feet above the ground, freefalling through the blue sky and white clouds, then sailing down under a winglike parachute. Today's sports parachutes are custom-built, state-of-the-art, lightweight, and comfortable. Parachutists can jump using one of three methods: static-line, accelerated freefall, or tandem fall.

Air Ventures (member, U.S. Parachute Association)
Gilmer County Airport
Rome, GA 30165
706-234-3087

Air Ventures offers a full range of all types of skydiving. The school provides instruction to earn a USPA license, which is required for anyone who is solo jumping. All schooling, parachutes, equipment, aircraft, and a drop zone are provided. Before a tandem jump, you must complete a 45-minute ground school. For a static-line jump, the mandatory training is six hours. The minimum age to participate is sixteen to seventeen with parental permission.

SPELUNKING

The Georgia/Alabama/Tennessee Region has the largest concentration of caves in the nation and is the site of the national headquarters of the National Speleological Society. Local chapters are called Grottos. Georgia's chapter, the Dogwood City Grotto, is one of the most active in the country. For more information, contact:

National Speleological Society
Cave Avenue
Huntsville, AL 35810
205-852-1300.

TREE CLIMBING

Treeclimbers International
P.O. Box 5588
Atlanta, GA 30307-5588

The motto of recreational tree climbing is "Get high! Climb trees." Local clubs are called Groves, and the founding Grove

195

is in Atlanta—America's most heavily forested major city. Members get networking, mentoring, and instruction, using ropes, harnesses, and other climbing gear. In fact, techniques are drawn from rock climbing, caving, and the arborist profession. The two basic tenets of tree climbing are safety and good stewardship. For example, climbers do not use the leg-spikes employed by pole climbers because of damage to the trees. Grove-sponsored classes are offered every other week as well as regular climbs and camping trips. Advanced climbers participate in such activities as tree surfing and flying traverses. Membership in a Grove also includes a newsletter.

WATERSKIING WITHOUT A BOAT

Ski Rixen
P.O. Box 3203
Jekyll Island, GA 31520
912-635-3802

A unique overhead cable system makes waterskiing without a boat possible. Called cableskiing, the process tows skiers quietly around a manmade lake at speeds to suit every thrill-seeker from beginner to advanced. Lessons are provided for all levels of experience. Beginners start on kneeboards; advanced skiers may do double or trick skis, slalom or barefoot skiing.

WILDERNESS SCHOOL

Atlanta Outward Bound
310 North McDonough Street

Decatur, GA 30030
404-378-0494

Atlanta Outward Bound designs programs for students in grades six through eight in the Atlanta city schools and grades six through 10 in the Decatur city schools. Outward Bound works with classroom teachers to see that programs pertinent to classwork, such as science and math, meet the Outward Bound criteria for building self-esteem, teamwork, and cooperation. Experiences range from an afternoon of urban exploration to a six- to eight-day wilderness experience. Subjects covered include compass skills and map reading.

Eagle Adventure Company
P.O. Box 970
McCaysville, GA 30555
800-288-3245

A yearly youth retreat includes team building and group skills learned through a variety of outdoor adventures such as swimming, rafting, rappelling, horseback riding, hiking, and other less strenuous activities, including gold panning, a hayride, and a bonfire.

Medicine Bow
Route 4, Box 1342
Wahsega Road
Dahlonega, GA 30533
706-864-5928

Medicine Bow instructors teach survival skills to both adults and children in a weekend workshop that stresses the secrets of Native Americans in using the forest as an asset to staying alive comfortably. You'll learn how to carry less gear, as well as tips on shelter, fire, food, cooking, and attitude.

Wolfcreek Wilderness School
2158 West Wolfcreek Road
Blairsville, GA 30512
706-745-5553
Contact: Naomi Ross, Executive Director

Wolfcreek Wilderness School, located in the North Georgia mountains, was established in 1972 as a nonprofit service organization to provide an alternative to traditional learning methods and foster an awareness of the interrelationship between man and nature. Instructors can tailor programs for school groups, families, or corporations.

Participants stay at rustic Wolfcreek Lodge, which has dorm-style sleeping facilities, a dining hall, living room with fireplace, conference room, kitchen, and bath facilities. The thirty-acre complex, adjacent to the Chattahoochee National Forest, features ropes courses, trails, and ponds. The Ropes Course is constructed from steel cables, wood, and live trees. The low ropes course develops trust and cooperation skills, while the high ropes courses consist of noncompetitive exercises.

Other activities of the school include canoeing, backpacking, rock climbing, spelunking, and primitive camping. Trips away from the school include sea kayaking.

11

SPECIAL PLACES

The following places offer a variety of outdoor recreational options. The locations are described here; sites are also included in chapters on specific activities.

AUGUSTA CANAL

Augusta Canal Authority
801 Broad Street, Room 507
Augusta, GA 30901
706-722-1071

The Augusta Canal is a National Historic Landmark used by hikers, bikers, canoers, fishermen, and environmentalists. Years ago the canal was used during the week for transporting people, materials, and cotton and on weekends was used as a recreational waterway for picnics and other leisure pursuits. From the beginning the canal was used for social events and as an escape from the city. In the 1840s, boats charged fifty cents to take passengers up the canal. All-day lock parties were popular entertainment well into the twentieth century. Today events are held at the dance pavilion, barbecue pit, and picnic shelter.

When Gen. James Oglethorpe founded Augusta in 1736, he recognized that to use the Savannah River fully, a lock system was needed at the Bull Sluice rapids—the fall line between the Piedmont plateau and the coastal plain. The goal was to provide easier access to the city for barges of cotton and other produce from the western counties, to furnish power for industrial development, and to bring water into Augusta. However, it was not until 1845 that construction began on the canal, using slaves, freed blacks, and Irish crews as laborers. It was opened in 1846 when the seven-mile first level was completed. The second and third levels were finished in 1848, bringing the canal's full length to nine miles.

Farmers shipped cotton down river in narrow Petersburg boats. When the barges reached the 13th Street Basin, cotton was loaded onto wagons and transported to the warehouses of Cotton Row on Reynolds Street. By 1850, 25,000 bales were passing through Augusta annually.

The City Council took over ownership of the canal in 1849. From 1872 to 1875, 200 imported Chinese workers worked to enlarge the canal. Many of them settled in Augusta, where their descendants form the city's present-day prosperous Chinese community. Various other changes were made on the canal up until the 1930s.

The old towpath where the mules towed the barges up and down the canal provides hiking, biking, and nature walks. In 1773, the naturalist William Bartram explored along the river, recording many of the indigenous plants in his journal. Today many of these plants still thrive along the canal, as well as giant loblolly pines, cypress, winged elm, sugarberry, sweet gum, patch-barked sycamore, and oak. In the trees you'll see mistletoe and Spanish moss.

At the water's edge, you'll find submerged and semi-submerged water plants such as elodea, parrot feather, bulrushes, and cattails. Creepers include trumpet creeper vine, honeysuckle, and, unfortunately, poison ivy.

Wildlife includes kingfishers, geese, osprey, beaver, river otter, deer, wild turkey, bald eagle, wood stork, great blue heron, green heron, loons, banded water snakes, yellow-bellied slider turtles, alligators, bobcats, cotton-mouth moccasins, and raccoons.

The fish ladder allows striped bass, hybrid bass, white bass, and American shad to continue upriver to their spawning grounds, providing good fishing year-round. Other common fish are black bass, yellow perch, catfish, shellcracker, bluegill, redbreasted bream, and longnose and spotted gar.

A levee, separate from the canal bank, that runs for seven miles along the canal is another easy place to walk or ride a bike. Part of the levee is incorporated into the Riverwalk Park, a complex of shops, restaurants, an outdoor amphitheater, a hotel, and an art museum.

The Clearing is a landing for bikers, hikers, and canoers and is popular for picnics. There's also a canoe portage between the canal and the Savannah River.

In addition to dams, gates, locks, spillways, and Lakes Warren and Olmstead, historical sites along the canal include notable houses, schools, and churches of the period as well as springhouses, the 1899 pumping station, the aqueduct, several mills, and the Confederate States Powder Works Chimney.

The 168-foot chimney is all that's left of the Powder Works, the only permanent structure begun and completed by the Confederacy. Augusta was chosen as the site of the powderworks because of its central location, canal transportation, water power, railroad facilities, and security from attack. Although the factory was torn down after the war, the chimney remains. A plaque recognizes the chimney "as a fitting monument to the dead heroes who sleep on the unnumbered battlefields of the South."

CHATTAHOOCHEE RIVER NATIONAL RECREATION AREA

Superintendent
National Park Service
1978 Island Ford Parkway
Dunwoody, GA 30350
404-394-7912, 394-8335, or 952-4419

Along the banks of the Chattahoochee River flowing through Atlanta, the Chattahoochee Recreation Area offers forty-eight miles of recreational activities. The water is usually clear, cold, and slow moving, but it can become a muddy torrent after storms or if water has been released from Lake Lanier upstream. Favorite pastimes include rafting, canoeing, kayaking, rowing, fishing, hiking, mountain biking, horseback riding, and wildlife observation. In addition to fishing and hiking, which are available at all the units, specific sections of the park offer other facilities, as listed.

Abbotts Bridge near Duluth—boat launch, picnic area
Cochran Shoals near Marietta—fitness activity trail, picnic area, rest rooms
Gold Branch near Roswell—picnic area

202

Island Ford in Dunwoody—park headquarters, rest rooms, ranger station

Johnson Ferry near Marietta—boat launch, picnic area, raft rental, shuttle bus

Jones Bridge near Alpharetta—boat launch, picnic area, rest rooms

Medlock Bridge near Norcross—boat launch, picnic area

Morgan Falls Dam near Sandy Springs—boat launch

Paces Mill near Marietta—ranger station, picnic area, boat launch, rest rooms, raft rental, shuttle bus

Palisades near Marietta—overlook, ranger station, rest rooms

Powers Island near Marietta—boat launch, raft rental, shuttle bus, restrooms

Sope Creek near Marietta—no facilities

Suwannee Creek near Duluth—no facilities

Vickery Creek in Roswell—picnic area

Exercise special caution on the river. Currents can be strong around submerged rocks and jagged tree snags or if water is released upstream. Wear rubber-soled shoes because of slippery rocks and the possibility of broken glass. A Coast Guard–approved life preserver is required for each person in a canoe, kayak, or raft. Wear lightweight, quick-drying clothes in warm weather, but wool in cool weather. Never dive into the river. Submerged rocks, murky water, and fluctuating water levels make diving very dangerous. In fact, swimming is not recommended.

Camping is not permitted in the park, nor open campfires. Fires are allowed only in picnic grills or portable stoves. Pets must be on a leash. Firearms, hunting, and metal detectors are prohibited. Climbing on ruins is not permitted. Glass containers are prohibited on the river between Morgan Falls

Dam and Paces Mill. Alcohol consumption is not permitted on land or water in the Jones Bridge Unit and in the Roswell Dam area of the Vickery Creek Unit. Mountain biking is permitted in some units. Horses are permitted on most paths, but proof of a negative Coggins test is required for every horse entering the areas. It is best to call ahead and make arrangements before visiting.

The park is a unit of the National Park System administered by the National Park Service, U.S. Department of the Interior.

For river conditions, call Buford Dam, 404-945-1466, or Morgan Falls Dam, 404-329-1455.

CUMBERLAND ISLAND NATIONAL SEASHORE

National Park Service
P.O. Box 806
St. Marys, GA 31558
912-882-4335

This unspoiled island boasts twenty miles of wide, flat, hard-packed undeveloped beach that seems to stretch out endlessly, backed by acres heavily wooded with live oak and palmetto. Wildlife includes birds, alligators, deer, wild horses, and sea turtles, to name just a few.

The human history of the island spans 4,000 years. Piles of midden shells indicate Native American settlers, who called the island "Missoe," or sassafras. Spanish soldiers and missionaries inhabited the island in the 1500s. Long-gone Fort William and Fort St. Andrews protected British interests during the Revolutionary War. After that war, Gen. Nathanael Greene purchased property and his widow constructed a tabby home she called Dungeness. In the 1890s a settlement was established for black workers. The zenith of opulence occurred around the turn of the century, when several members of the Carnegie family built lavish retreats on the island, but they eventually abandoned it.

In 1972, the island became a national seashore. Access is by ferry only. Visitors are limited to 300 campers and day-trippers per day. No vehicles are permitted except those of residents. Camping is available at a campground and at primitive sites. Visitors can enjoy the beach as well as fishing, hiking, wildlife observations, and certain remains of the Carnegie estates.

While most of the remains are too dangerous to be toured, the 1898 Georgian Revival mansion called Plum Orchard is in excellent condition, and much of the original furniture remains. As funds become available it is being restored. Occasional tours are given.

An ideal alternative for the visitor who disdains primitive camping is the privately owned **Greyfield Inn**. The luxurious turn-of-the-century mansion sits on 1,300 acres with access to the beach and is still operated by descendants of the Carnegies. You'll be assured a pampered stay with gourmet dining. Transportation to and from Fernandina Beach, Florida, is provided aboard the inn's private ferry. Call 904-261-6408 or contact Greyfield Inn at 8 North Second Street, Fernandina Beach, FL 32035-0900.

ATLANTA AREA

Fulton County Parks and Recreation
1575 Northside Drive, N.W.

Atlanta, GA 30318
404-730-6200

The largest county in the state, the metro Atlanta county of Fulton boasts an outstanding park system, including the following multiuse parks:

Boatrock Recreation Center, Atlanta
Chattahoochee River Park, Roswell
Clarence Duncan Park, Fairburn
Cliftondale Park, College Park
Hammond Park and Community Center, Sandy Springs
Providence Outdoor Recreation Center, Alpharetta
Red Oak Recreation Center, College Park
Rico Recreation Center, Palmetto
Sandtown Park, Atlanta
Welcome All Park, College Park
Wilkerson Mill–Farris Park, Palmetto
Wills Park, Alpharetta

Equestrian Activities

Wills Park Equestrian Center, Alpharetta

Nature Reserves/Centers

Autrey Mill Nature Preserve, Alpharetta
Chattahoochee Nature Center, Roswell
Cochran Mill Park, Palmetto

Programs for Special Populations

South Fulton Therapeutics, Cliftondale Park, College Park
Special Recreational Services Center, Atlanta

Tennis

Burdett Tennis Center, College Park
North Fulton Tennis Center, Sandy Springs
South Fulton Tennis Center, College Park

Trap and Skeet

Wolf Creek Trap & Skeet, Atlanta (site for the '96 Olympics shooting events)

Tours

Sandy Springs Historic Site, Sandy Springs

LITTLE ST. SIMONS ISLAND

Little St. Simons Island
P.O. Box 1078
St. Simons, GA 31522
912-638-7472
Contact: Deborah McIntyre

Providing relief from the everyday world, the privately owned barrier island Little St. Simons lies adjacent to heavily developed St. Simons and is accessible only by a twice-daily private ferry. While the Berolzheimer family uses the island much of the year, there are certain periods when it is open to overnight guests. The 10,000-acre island caters to a maximum of only twenty-four guests at a time with a staff of seventeen, including two full-time naturalists and an intern, a stable manager, fishing and boating guides, and an outstanding kitchen staff.

You need your camera and maybe a good pair of binoculars. The island is a photographer's dream.

Unspoiled beaches yield fists full of sand dollars and other shells. A word to the wise: these beaches are completely natural. They aren't raked and cleared of the flotsam that the ocean deposits there each day.

The island harbors seven nesting pairs of wood storks and is one of the few completely protected nesting grounds for sea turtles. Freely roaming deer, soaring eagles, pristine forests, freshwater ponds, isolated beaches, marshlands, and over 200 species of birds, including egrets, wood stork, heron, and red-winged blackbirds, are among the major attractions. Glimpses of gators, armadillos, and snakes provide some excitement.

Every day several guided naturalist activities—such as hunting for turtle eggs—will be listed, but you can get one of the naturalists to go out with you if you want to examine some specific flora or fauna.

Horseback riding is offered early in the morning or late in the afternoon. You'll be matched up with a mount that suits your experience level.

Canoeing, fishing, long walks, swimming in the ocean or pool, kayak lessons, croquet, and boccie ball tournaments are other diversions. The resort has several flat-bottomed fishing boats with trolling motors that are ideal for exploring the maze of hidden waterways in and around the island. The guides will take you out to their favorite spot if they aren't busy, or direct you to them otherwise. If you forget your fishing gear or don't want to get your freshwater tackle gummed up with salt, the resort has a fair assortment of equipment you can borrow. If you don't want to fish, you can take a boat out to do a little exploring. If you're not back by a certain time, someone will come looking for you.

Reflecting the almost 100-year history as a private retreat, the conglomeration of small dwellings represents a century of architectural styles. At one end of the continuum, the
Hunting Lodge and several other buildings are old and rustic,
circa 1917. The most recent additions include two lodges,
Cedar House and River House, built in the 1980s. Other buildings fill in the intervening years.

Screened porches with rockers and large wraparound
decks enable you to enjoy the delightful breeze, the river and
marsh panoramas, and spectacular sunsets in almost any
weather.

The Hunting Lodge houses the office, several common
rooms, and the dining room. It's filled with books and
memorabilia—old photos, pictures of the family, candid shots
of former guests Jimmy Carter and Walter Mondale, racks of
antlers, navigational charts, a Pony Express pouch, and a
rattlesnake skin. The lodge is comfortably furnished in old
wicker.

In addition to meals served in the dining room, ample
portions of home-cooked meals are sometimes served in the
screened pool house. A picnic at the beach at least once a
week is a much-anticipated event.

This island hideaway is ideal for family reunions, small
groups, or business conferences. In fact, from June through
August, the island is available only to groups who take the
entire complex.

Spring and fall are a perfect time to visit, and that's when
Little St. Simons is open to individuals, couples, families, and
very small groups—March through June 2 and October 1
through mid-November.

A stay at Little St. Simons is expensive, approximately
$300 per night. However, everything except drinks is included
in the price. There is even a grass landing strip for small

209

planes for guests who prefer to fly in. A two-night minimum is required because the owners feel you couldn't possibly relax and truly enjoy this paradise in only one day.

The only disadvantage we can see to Little St. Simons is that the beach is quite a distance from the lodge, which is located on the landward side of the island. It's really too far to walk out and back unless you really enjoy lots of walking. A pickup truck with benches in the back serves as a shuttle several times a day. Unfortunately, using the shuttle ties you down to certain hours—although some guests choose to ride one way and walk the other. Facilities at the beach are minimal; a large covered pavilion allows you to get out of the sun.

OKEFENOKEE NATIONAL WILDLIFE REFUGE

U.S. Fish and Wildlife Service
Okefenokee National Wildlife Refuge
Route 2, Box 338
Folkston, GA 31537
912-496-3331

Best known because of the comic-strip character Pogo and from serving as the locale of many Hollywood horror movies, "the land of the trembling earth" offers visitors 107 miles of canoe trails as well as camping, guided boat tours, hiking, wildlife observation, and more.

Once covered by the Atlantic Ocean, the area became a great lake. Now a primeval swamp, the Okefenokee features a 400,000-acre ecosystem containing islands, lakes, forested and nonforested terrain, and lily pad prairies, all of which provide wildlife sanctuaries for endangered species. Visitors can expect to see alligators, sand cranes, bear, raccoons, and sun-fish. Plants include orchids, water lilies, red sundew, and ferns.

Access to the swamp is at three entrances: East-Folkston, West-Fargo, and North-Waycross.

The Folkston entrance features a visitors center, concession center, boat launching, picnic area, canoe trails, hiking trails, Chesser Island homestead, observation tower, a day-use shelter with restrooms, and an overnight shelter with rest-rooms. For more information, contact either the superin-tendent's office listed above or:

Carl Glenn, Jr., Concessionaire
Okefenokee National Wildlife Refuge
Suwannee Canal Recreation Concession, Inc.
Route 2, Box 336
Folkston, GA 31537
912-496-7156

The Fargo entrance features tent and trailer camping sites, an interpretive center, picnic shelters, cottages, boat rental, guided boat tours, and annual special events. Contact:

Stephen C. Foster State Park
(a primary entrance to the swamp)
Route 1, Box 131
Fargo, GA 31631
912-637-5274

The Waycross entrance is the site of Okefenokee Swamp Park, a private enterprise featuring a serpentarium and wildlife observatory, Swamp Creation Center, Living Swamp

Center, a swamp homestead, and guided boat tours. Contact:

Okefenokee Swamp Park
Waycross, GA 31501
912-283-0583

STATE PARKS AND MORE

Georgia's State Parks and Historic Sites
205 Butler Street, S.E., Suite 1258
Atlanta, GA 30334
404-656-3530
Toll free in Georgia, 800-342-7275
Toll free outside Georgia, 800-542-7275
Georgia boasts fifty-eight state parks and historic sites, blanketing the state from the ocean to the highest mountain peak. These parks provide camping, hiking, fishing, boating, and biking. Some even feature golf courses. Many also provide accommodations in lodges and cottages.

A Georgia Parkpass is required for parked vehicles in state parks. Visitors pay a daily parking fee or may purchase an annual parking pass. The Parkpass is valid at all state parks visited the same day. You can buy an annual Parkpass at all parks and historic sites. Guests in lodges, cottages, and campgrounds pay one fee for the duration of their stay. Wednesdays are free days for day-use visitors. A senior citizen (age sixty-two and older) annual Parkpass is also available. Fees are used for repairing and maintaining state parks.

12 ORGANIZATIONS AND PROVIDERS

Atlanta Oceans
993 Northrope Drive
Atlanta, GA 30324

The environmentally conscious members of Atlanta Oceans actively participate in the preservation and protection of oceans, rivers, and other waterways as well as marine and other wildlife. The group sponsors both in-state and out-of-state trips, such as a river clean-up, sea turtle rescue, or manatee watch. An annual Chili Cookoff raises funds for Save the Manatee Club. Membership includes a monthly newsletter.

PATH Foundation
P.O. Box 14327
Atlanta, GA 30324
404-355-6438

People in Atlanta for Trails Here is a nonprofit organization working to develop a pedestrian and bicycle trail system in metro Atlanta. The foundation believes that such a system will reduce pollution and congestion, spawn new recreational opportunities by linking the city's major parks, and provide safety for joggers, cyclists, and hikers. When complete, the system will connect Georgia Tech, Stone Mountain, the Arts districts, Greenbriar Mall, and the Chattahoochee River. The organization will assemble corridors, acquire rights-of-way, oversee construction of trails, and assist in setting up a maintenance program.

In addition to walking and planning proposed trail routes, membership includes parties, staffing booths at local events, distributing literature, soliciting new members, developing publicity, and fundraising.

Singles Outdoor Adventures Club
P.O. Box 6234
Marietta, GA 30065-0234

This club meets monthly and features speakers on such topics as canoeing, tubing, hiking, whitewater rafting, camping, biking, and sailing. Numerous field trips and social events are held throughout the year.

MULTISPORT ACTIVITIES ORGANIZATIONS
(More information about each can be found in chapters on specific sports.)

Eagle Adventure Company
P.O. Box 970

McCaysville, GA 30555
800-288-3245

Located in the North Georgia mountains straddling the Georgia/Tennessee/North Carolina border, Eagle Adventure Company offers fly-fishing expeditions, llama trekking, gold panning, hayrides, hiking, horseback riding, overnight horseback riding, rappelling, tubing, white-water rafting, caving, and a youth wilderness school.

Fulton County Parks and Recreation
1575 Northside Drive N.W.
Atlanta, GA 30318
404-730-6200

Atlanta is located in Fulton County. At seventy miles long, Fulton is by far the largest county in the state, and it boasts the finest public park system we've ever seen. In addition to numerous multi-use parks, the county offers several special-purpose ones: Burdett, North Fulton, and South Fulton Tennis Centers; Special Recreational Services Center and South Fulton Therapeutics, which both offer programs for special populations; Chattahoochee, Cochran Mill, and Autrey Mill Nature Centers; Providence Outdoor Recreation Center; Wolf Creek Trap & Skeet Range, and Wills Park Equestrian Center. Most of these facilities are explained in more detail in the appropriate chapter.

Georgia Wildlife Adventures, Inc.
404-978-0624
Contact: Tim Zech

Georgia Wildlife Adventures specializes in outdoor activities throughout the state. The guide service can arrange anything from trout fishing in the North Georgia mountains to wild boar hunting in South Georgia. Other activities include horseback riding, white-water rafting, skeet and trap shooting, and hiking.

The service is particularly popular with out-of-town visitors because Tim Zech will pick you up from your hotel, transport you to the site of your adventure, provide all necessary equipment and supplies, and return you to your hotel.

Medicine Bow
Route 8, Box 1780/Wahsega Road
Dahlonega, GA 30533
706-864-5928

Medicine Bow is a primitive school of earthlore in the North Georgia mountains. The outdoor school for all ages connects ancient skills and Native American lore to skills such as sources of food, medicine, tools, fire, art, shelter, and comfort. The organization offers seasonal workshops, summer camp, archery, canoeing, camping, nature study, and Native American ceremonies.

Spartina Trails, Inc.
P.O. Box 2531
Savannah, GA 31402
912-234-4621

The guides at Spartina Trails offer exploratory tours of Georgia's barrier islands. You can eavesdrop on the underwater conversations of dolphins and other sea creatures using hydrophones. Other activities include hiking onshore, bird watching along the coast, and fishing using a seine net.

Activities are under the guidance of naturalist Cathy Sakas, writer/host of public television's "The Coastal Naturalist" series.

Wilderness Southeast
711 Sandtown Road
Savannah, GA 31410-1019
912-897-5108

Wilderness Southeast offers study tours as well as camping, canoeing/kayaking, photography, and wildlife observation on its three- and four-day Okefenokee Swamp tours, four-day sea kayaking trips, five-day sea turtle watch, and four- to six-day Cumberland Island expeditions. The company also offers science summer camps for middle-schoolers.

13

SOURCES OF INFORMATION

Whether you are a longtime Georgia resident, a recent transplant, a visitor, or a potential visitor, by far the single best compendium of information is the state travel guide *Georgia on My Mind*. It describes the highlights to be found in each of the state's nine tourism regions and then lists hundreds of attractions, lodgings, and restaurants. Also included are a Georgia road map and a matrix of the facilities at each of Georgia's State Parks and Historic Sites. The guide is available free from the Georgia Department of Industry, Trade and Tourism (see "State Agencies" below).

VISITOR INFORMATION AND WELCOME CENTERS

The next best source for a wealth of information on what the state has to offer is a visit to a state-funded Georgia Visitor Information Center, located at the state borders along the interstate highway system. The primary centers are at the north-south entries on I-75, I-85, and I-95 and the east-west entries on I-16 and I-20.

Each center offers one-stop shopping—racks hold hundreds of brochures on federal, state, and private tourist attractions within Georgia, as well as material about meals and lodging. Naturally, each center has more data on the particular area in which it is located, but they do carry statewide information. Unfortunately, due to lack of funds and the quantity of material they carry, these centers are unable to mail information to you.

In addition to the state centers, many towns and counties have local welcome centers. The material available at smaller centers is more area-specific, and they are more likely to be able to mail information to you.

Following is a list of information and welcome centers arranged by tourist region. Those starred (*) are state centers; the others are local.

ATLANTA METRO

Atlanta History Center
Local Welcome Center
140 Peachtree Street
Atlanta, GA 30301
404-238-0655

Atlanta Airport Visitors
Information Center*
Airport Branch
Atlanta, GA 30320
404-767-3231

Atlanta Local Welcome
Center—Lenox Square Mall
3393 Peachtree Road, N.E.
Atlanta, GA 30326
404-266-1398

Atlanta Local Welcome
Center—Peachtree Center
233 Peachtree Street, N.E.
Atlanta, GA 30303
404-521-6688

**Atlanta Welcome Center—
Underground Atlanta**
Pryor & Alabama Streets
Atlanta, GA 30303
404-577-2148

**Clayton County Local
Welcome Center**
8712 Tara Boulevard
Jonesboro, GA 30237
404-478-6549

Classic South

**Georgia Visitors
Information Center—
Martinez***
I-20
Martinez, GA 30917
(706) 737-1446

**Historic Roswell
Convention & Visitors
Center**
617 South Atlanta Street
Roswell, GA 30075
404-640-3253

Marietta Welcome Center
No. 4 Depot Street
Marietta, GA 30060
404-429-1115

**Augusta Local
Welcome Center**
8th & Reynolds
(Riverwalk/Cotton
    Exchange Building)
Augusta, GA 30913
706-724-4067 or 800-
    726-0243

Colonial Coast

**Brunswick–Golden Isles
Local Welcome Center**
I-95 between Exits 8 & 9
Brunswick, GA 31520
912-264-0202 or 800-
    933-COAST

**Brunswick–Golden Isles
Local Welcome Center**
Glynn Avenue on US 17
Brunswick, GA 31520
912-264-5337 and 800-
    933-COAST

Darien–McIntosh County Local Welcome Center
US 17 at Darien River Bridge
Darien, GA 31305
912-437-4192 or 437-6684

Darien–McIntosh County Welcome Center
I-95, Exit 11
Eulonia, GA 31331
912-832-4444, ext. 721

Georgia Visitor Information Center—Kingsland*
I-95
Kingsland, GA 31548
912-729-3253

Georgia Visitor Information Center—Garden City*
I-95
Garden City, GA 31418
912-964-5094

Jekyll Island Local Welcome Center
901 Jekyll Causeway
Jekyll Island, GA 31527
912-635-3636 or 800-841-6586

St. Marys Welcome Center
Orange Hall
Osborne Street
St. Marys, GA 31558
912-882-4000

Savannah Local Welcome Center—Downtown
301 Martin Luther King
 Boulevard
Savannah, GA 31401
912-944-0456 or 800-444-2427

Tybee Island Welcome Center
209 Butler Avenue
Tybee Island, GA 31328
912-786-5444

Historic Heartland

Athens
Local Welcome Center
280 East Dougherty Street
Athens, GA 30603
706-353-1820

Eagle Tavern
Local Welcome Center
US 411
Watkinsville, GA 30677
706-769-5197

Macon I-16
Local Welcome Center
200 Cherry Street
Macon, GA 31201
912-743-3401

Macon I-75
Local Welcome Center
I-75 South
Macon, GA 31208
912-745-2668

Perry
Local Welcome Center
101 Courtney Hodges
Boulevard
Perry, GA 31069
912-988-8000

Magnolia Midlands

Baxley
Local Welcome Center
501 West Parker Street
US 301
Baxley, GA 31513
912-367-7731

Claxton
Local Welcome Center
4 North Duval Street
U S 301

Claxton, GA 30417
912-739-2281

Eastman
Local Welcome Center
407 College Street
Eastman, GA 31203
912-374-4723

**Georgia Visitor
Information Center—
Sylvania***
US 301
Sylvania, GA 30467
912-829-3331

**Glennville
Local Welcome Center**
134 S. Main Street
US 301
Glennville, GA 30427
912-654-2000

**Metter
Local Welcome Center**
I-16 at Metter Exit 23

Northeast Mountains

**Gainesville
Local Welcome Center**
230 East Butler Parkway
Gainesville, GA 30501
706-532-6206

**Dahlonega–Lumpkin
County Local Welcome
Center**
Public Square
Dahlonega, GA 30533
706-864-3711

Metter, GA 30439
912-685-6151

**Million Pines
Local Welcome Center**
I-16 at Soperton Exit 29
Soperton, GA 30457
912-529-6263

**Reidsville
Local Welcome Center**
US 280, Brazell Street
Reidsville, GA 30453
912-557-6323

**Greater Helen
Local Welcome Center**
Main Street
Helen, GA 30545
706-878-2521

**Georgia Visitor
Information Center—
Lavonia***
I-85
Lavonia, GA 30553
706-356-4019

Rabun County
Local Welcome Center
US 441
Clayton, GA 30525
706-782-5113

Northwest Mountains

Acworth Welcome Center
Exit 120 off I-75 and State 92
Acworth, GA 30101
404-974-7626

Blue Ridge Visitor Center
Historic Depot
P.O. Box 875
Blue Ridge, GA 30513
706-632-5680

Calhoun
Local Welcome Center
300 South Wall Street
Calhoun, GA 30701
706-625-3200

Plantation Trace

Albany
Local Welcome Center
225 West Broad Street
Albany, GA 31701
912-434-8700

Toccoa–Stephens County
Local Welcome Center
907 East Currahee Street
Toccoa, GA 30571
706-886-2132

Chatsworth
Local Welcome Center
State 52
Chatsworth, GA 30705
706-695-6060

Douglasville
Local Welcome Center
P.O. Box 395
Douglasville, GA 30133
404-942-5022

Georgia Visitor
Information Center—
Ringgold*
I-75
Ringgold, GA 30736
706-937-4211

Thomasville–Thomas
County Local Welcome
Center
401 South Broad Street
Thomasville, GA 31792
912-226-9600

Georgia Visitor Information Center—Lake Park*
I-75
Lake Park, GA 31636
912-559-5828

Presidential Pathways

Andersonville Welcome Center
Old Railroad Depot
Andersonville, GA 31711
912-924-2558

Georgia Visitors Information Center— Columbus*
I-185 at Williams Road
Columbus, GA 31904
706-649-7455

Pine Mountain Welcome Center
101 Broad Street
Pine Mountain, GA 31822
800-441-3502

Georgia Visitors Information Center— Plains*
US 280
Plains, GA 31780
912-824-7477

Georgia Visitors Information Center— West Point*
I-85
West Point, GA 31833
706-645-3353

FEDERAL AGENCIES

National Park Service/Southeast Region
75 Spring Street, S.W., 10th Floor
Atlanta, GA 30303
404-331-5187

U.S. Army
Corps of Engineers
30 Pryor Street, S.W.
Atlanta, GA 30335-6801
404-331-6715

U.S. Fish and Wildlife
Service
75 Spring Street, S.W.,
    12th Floor

Richard B. Russell Building
Atlanta, GA 30303
404-331-6343

U.S. Forest Service
Information Center
1720 Peachtree Road, N.W.,
    Room 154
Atlanta, GA 30367-9102
404-347-2384

Specifically ask for "A Guide to the Chattahoochee-Oconee National Forests," which provides useful information about the facilities of each recreation area and directions for getting to each, as well as detailed information on the trail system. Also available from the Forest Service is "A Guide to Your National Forests." You can buy maps of all the National Forests in several formats: printed on offset paper, moisture-resistant paper, or water and tearproof paper.

STATE AGENCIES

Game and Fish Division
Georgia Department of Natural Resources
205 Butler Street, S.E.
Room 1362
Atlanta, GA 30334
404-656-3524

Publications you can get from the Georgia Department of Natural Resources include "Georgia State Parks and Historic Sites" and "Great Georgia Getaways."

Georgia Tourist Division
Georgia Department of Industry, Trade and Tourism
P.O. Box 1776
Atlanta, GA 30301
404-656-3590

In addition to information on the tourism regions, you can get these publications from the Georgia Tourism Division: "Georgia Bicycle Touring Guide"; "Georgia on My Mind," a state travel guide; "Fishing in Georgia"; "Camping in Georgia"; "Georgia Days," a listing of activities each quarter.

Department of Transportation
#2 Capitol Square
Atlanta, GA 30334
404-656-5267

Highway maps and road conditions.

Jekyll Island Authority
373 Riverview Drive
Jekyll Island, GA 31520
800-342-1042 in Georgia
800-841-6586 outside Georgia

OTHER AGENCIES

Lake Lanier Islands Authority
P.O. Box 605
Buford, GA 30518
404-945-6701

Stone Mountain Memorial Association
P.O. Box 778
Stone Mountain, GA 30086
404-498-5600

BOOKS

de Hart, Allen. *Adventuring in Florida and the Sea Islands and Okefenokee Swamp of Georgia.* San Francisco, CA: Sierra Club Books, 1991.

For information on bed and breakfast accommodations:
Thalimer, Carol and Dan. *Bed and Breakfast Inns of Georgia.* Atlanta, GA: Cherokee Press, 1994. (The only complete guide to B&B accommodations in the state.)

FISHING INFORMATION

For information on fishing and fishing methods, seasons, and exact locations, contact:

University of Georgia Marine Extension Service
UGA Marine Extension Station
P.O. Box Z
Brunswick, GA 31523
912-264-7268

"Coastal Georgia Fishing"
Coastal Georgia Regional Development Center
P.O. Box 1917
Brunswick, GA 31521
912-264-7363

Georgia Department of Natural Resources
Coastal Resources Division
1200 Glynn Avenue
Brunswick, GA 31523-9990
912-264-7218

INDEX

230